LINETTE HOGLUND

ILLUSTRATIONS BY GLENN WOLFF

A Fireside Book Published by Simon & Schuster Inc., New York   London   Toronto   Sydney   Tokyo

JEWEL LAKE

SEAFOOD MARKET

COOKBOOK

Copyright © 1988 by Linette Hoglund
Illustrations © 1988 by Glenn Wolff
A FIRESIDE BOOK
Published by Simon & Schuster Inc.
Simon & Schuster Building
Rockefeller Center
1230 Avenue of the Americas
New York, NY 10020
FIRESIDE and colophon are registered trademarks
of Simon & Schuster Inc.
Designed by Bonni Leon
Manufactured in the United States
of America
10 9 8 7 6 5 4 3 2 1
Library of Congress Cataloging in
Publication Data
Hoglund, Linette.
    The Jewel Lake Seafood Market Cookbook.

    "A Fireside book."
    Includes index.
    1. Cookery (Seafood)   2. Cookery—Alaska.   I. Title.
TX747.H635   1988   641.6'92   88-11537
ISBN 0-671-65697-X

ACKNOWLEDGMENTS

My deepest thanks to the following people: my mother, Suzy Hoglund, who encouraged my cooking interest; my father, Bill Hoglund, who night after night in Alaska tested my recipes; my sister, Laurie Hoglund, also a willing tester; and Jan Hoglund and Faith Hornby, who pushed me to write the book. Thanks also to Jim Maguire and the Maguire family for the use of their kitchen as well as their tastebuds.

Finally, a special thanks to my friends at the New York Stock Exchange who gave me lots of support: Jack Dalessandro, Mike Chiara, Patty Mirenda, and Herb Ruppenstein. And from First Boston Corporation—Teddy "G" and Jimmy Hennessy; from Paine Webber—Kevin Ludewick, Steve Codd, and John O'Neill; from E. F. Hutton—Jimmy MacMullen, Pat Marchese, and Rich Starsia; from Morgan Stanley—Jimmy McDermott, Jim Riley, Dudley Divine, Charlie Conolly, and Amy Chmura; from Drexel Burnham Lambert—Leesa Martin, Tom Nigro, Jim Ferris, and Jim Davis; and Scott Foster, Peter Henderson, and Bruce Meyer.

CONTENTS

FOREWORD

Alaska, "the last frontier," as many Americans refer to the forty-ninth state, is where I had the opportunity to live and work for a year and a half. My father owned a seafood store in Anchorage, Alaska, and a fishing boat that was docked out of the small town of Seward.

While running the seafood store, my wholesale business began to grow—I was catering to many of the local restaurants. I would hand-pick Alaskan king crab during the day for them and deliver it later in the afternoon. Many times I would stay in the back of the restaurant with the owners and staff, and learn, over a glass of wine, how to make salmon this way, or halibut another. I had a lot of fun and learned a lot about cooking.

Many of my retail customers would often ask the best way to prepare their seafood. At first I would jot down a recipe on a piece of scrap paper, but eventually I typed a few out, made copies, and left them on the counter. The demand for new recipes grew and I added new ones to my collection. That is how I compiled all the recipes for this book. I hope you enjoy them just as much as my Alaskan friends have.

Jewel Lake

SEAFOOD

MARKET

COOKBOOK

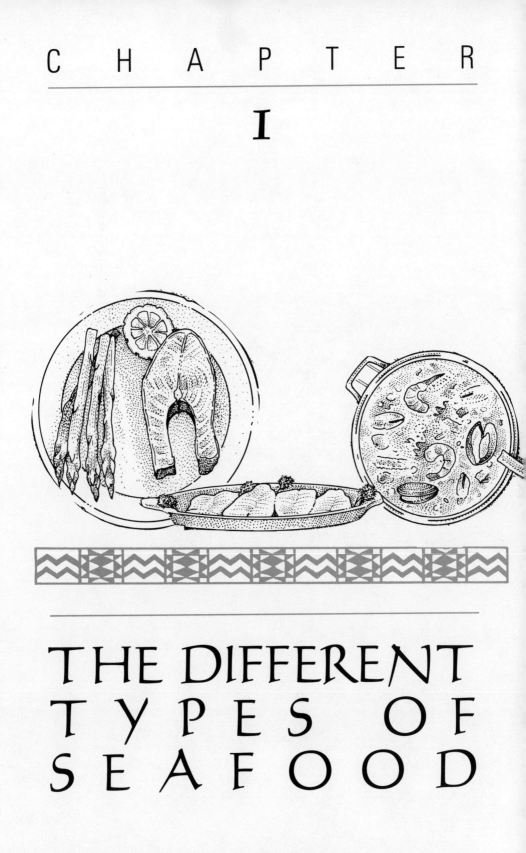

THE DIFFERENT TYPES OF SEAFOOD

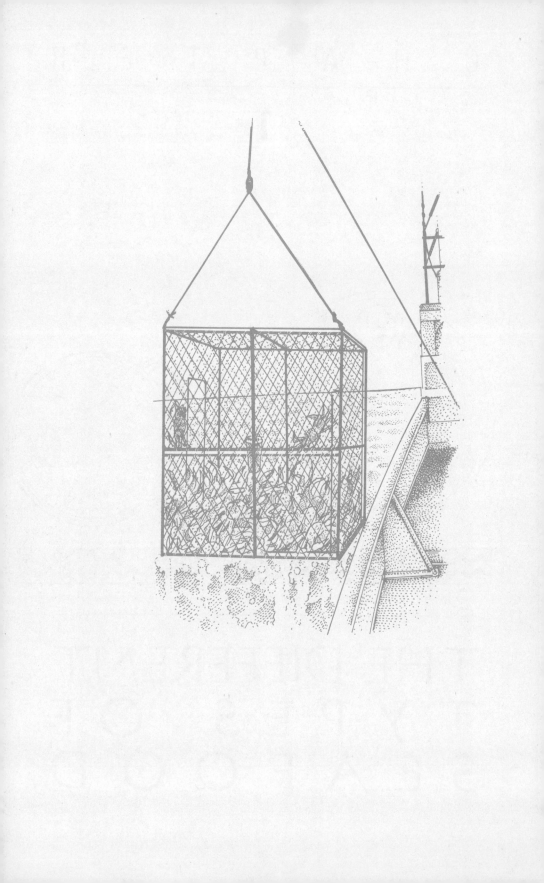

HOW TO TEST FOR FRESHNESS

On the following pages, I've given some information on the basic six types of seafood used in this cookbook. When buying fresh fish, remember these letters: G-E-T-S. Gills, Eyes, Texture, and Smell. This trick *gets* you the freshest fish.

GILLS: The gills of the fish should be bright red. If the gills are brown, the fish is not fresh.

EYES: The eyes should be clear, not cloudy.

TEXTURE: The flesh should be firm and elastic. It should bounce back when pressed.

SMELL: There should be very little smell. A pungent fishy odor, or one that smells of iodine, is a sign that the fish is not fresh.

SALMON

CHINOOK OR KING SALMON   is the most desirable and therefore most expensive salmon. It is pink, flavorful, and contains about 17 percent fat.

SOCKEYE OR RED SALMON   has red flesh and a slightly higher fat content than the Chinook. The gray area around and near the bone is fat.

COHO OR SILVER SALMON   has pink flesh and bright silver skin, with streaks of silver running down the tail fin.

DOG OR CHUM SALMON   is nearly fat-free, but the flesh color is yellowish-pink. This is not appealing looking and the flavor is not as good as coho salmon's flavor. You don't usually see chum salmon sold fresh in seafood stores; it is usually used for canned salmon meat.

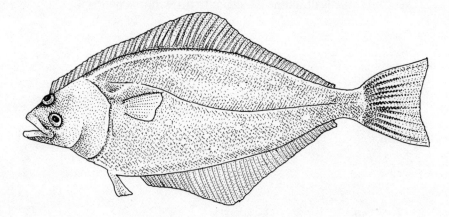

HALIBUT

You are unlikely to see the whole fish for sale but rather steaks, fillets, or roasts, because halibut range anywhere from ten pounds to several hundred pounds. So check for texture and smell.

The best time to purchase halibut is in the summer, but frozen halibut is hard to tell from the fresh and is available year-round.

CLAMS AND OYSTERS

CLAMS   There are hundreds of species of clams. However, we need only concern ourselves with the three basic varieties indigenous to our coastlines.

The first variety is called the *quahog* (pronounced ko'hog), the hard-shell clam. These small and delicate clams are more commonly known as *cherrystone* or *littleneck clams*.

The second type are a family of soft-shell clams known as *steamer clams*. This American favorite is most commonly steamed in a large pot with a small amount of water. They are served along with a bowl of clam broth and a bowl of drawn butter. The clam is first dipped in the clam broth for washing and then in the butter for flavor.

The third variety of clams include *surf clams* and *razor clams*. These clams are larger than all other types. Surf clams are also known as *giant clams* and are found on the East Coast of the United States. The razor clams, so named for its sharp edges, is a long, rectangular-shape clam found on the West Coast.

OYSTERS   come from waters along the Atalantic Coast, the Gulf of Mexico, and the Pacific Coast and vary a bit in shape and size. The Atlantic and Gulf oysters (known as *eastern oysters*) look somewhat like pear-shaped clams. The Pacific oysters come in two sizes—the smaller known as the *Olympia* and the larger known as the *Japanese* or *large Pacific oyster*—and has a curly rim on the outside of the oyster.

When buying oysters and clams, make sure their shells are tightly closed and are not broken or cracked. If you are buying the oysters or clams shucked, they should be elastic when fresh. If they are loose and mushy, they have been out of their shells too long.

When storing clams and oysters keep them on a plate losely wrapped with a damp kitchen towel in the refrigerator. Never submerge in plain water or they will suffocate.

CRABS

There are five types of crabs that we commonly use in America. Three of the five come from the ice-cold Pacific waters. They are *Alaskan king crab, Dungeness crab,* and *snow crab.*

Seafood stores will usually sell only the king crab legs, not the whole crab, already cooked and in their shells. Some stores may pick the large part of the leg—called "merus leg"—out of the shell and sell them separately. However, the large sections of the sweet meat are very expensive.

The Dungeness crabs are usually sold whole, cooked in the shell, or cooked and picked from the shell. When you buy a whole crab you take it home and clean it yourself, or ask your seafood store to do it for you. (It is very simple to clean a crab and something that I prefer to do myself.)

Snow crab has very long skinny legs and thin claws. The crab will be sold most often in seafood stores as cooked, picked crabmeat or canned.

The two types of Atlantic crabs are *blue crabs* and *stone crabs.* Blue crabs, which are abundant from Massachusetts to Florida, come in a hard shell and are usually sold alive, whole cooked or as cooked picked meat. The soft shell is found when the crab has shed its hard shell and has not yet developed its hard protective shell again.

Stone crabs are from Florida's waters and have a shell just like the name suggests. Its enamel-like shell takes a bit of effort to crack but is well worth the effort. The large claws are the only part of the crab that the fisherman will remove, then the crab is returned to the water to grow another claw. Stone crabs are always cooked in your seafood store. The crab will most often be served chilled with a lemon wedge and a fresh mustard mayonnaise sauce.

SCALLOPS

There are only two principal scallops used in the United States, *sea scallops* and *bay scallops*. The difference between the two is size and taste. Sea scallops, the larger of the two, run approximately ten to twenty per pound. The taste seems to be a bit stronger than that of bay scallops and lacks a little of the sweetness. The smaller bay scallops run approximately thirty-five to forty-five scallops to a pound, and are more mild in taste than sea scallops. However, due to size, when cooking scallops, the sea scallops retain a smooth center, while the bay scallops' center, being smaller, is not as easy to taste. Many "gourmets" will pay a higher price for the tiny bay scallops, although I prefer the taste, texture, and size of the sea scallop. Both types, when cooked right, are a gastronomic delight.

Scallops should never be stored in water. This increases their size and decreases their flavor. They should be stored in an airtight container and rinsed as little as possible. Look for a nice milky translucent color, not one of bright white (a sign that they have been soaked in water), and a glossy wet appearance, never dry.

SHRIMP

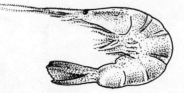

Shrimp, also known as *prawns, langoustine,* or *scampi* depending on where you are from, come in many different sizes and vary a bit in shape, color and taste.

In most seafood stores you will find the shrimp have been frozen, even though they do not look like it. A popular shrimp sold is the gulf shrimp. You may buy them in the shell as well as peeled and deveined. Shrimp are sold by the count—ten to fifteen in a pound (extra large), sixteen to twenty (large), twenty-one to twenty-five (medium), twenty-six to thirty (medium-small), thirty-one to thirty-five (small), and onto eighty to one hundred twenty as tiny *popcorn shrimp* or *cocktail shrimp.* Any shrimp fewer than ten to a pound are known as *jumbo shrimp,* many of which come from the Orient, especially Taiwan, where some shrimp can run two to a pound. There is a rule of thumb as far as shrimp prices go, the larger the shrimp, the higher the price.

When making a shrimp dinner, remember that two-and-one-half pounds of shrimp in the shell are equal to only one pound for shelled shrimp, and you will need one-quarter pound of shelled shrimp per person.

The shrimp should look plump, the tails bright orange or red, not black or brown. The eggs, if any, should not be mushy or dark. Most important, the meat should be firm to the touch, clear, not cloudy or white in color. Shrimp have a tendency to have a strong odor because of their high salt content, so don't let that bother you. However, if they reek of an odor similar to that of ammonia, which develops when the shrimp have been out in the air too long, they have turned rancid.

SEAFOOD SUBSTITUTION LIST

The fish used in this cookbook may be substituted with many other kinds. Here is a list to suggest some possibilities.

FOR SALMON AND HALIBUT:

BASS—STRIPED AND BLACK	RED SNAPPER
BLUEFISH	SHARK
COD	SOLE—ENGLISH, DOVER, GRAY
DOLPHIN	AND LEMON
FLOUNDER	SWORDFISH
GROUPER	TROUT
HADDOCK	TUNA
MONKFISH	WALLEYE
POMPANO	WHITEFISH

When substituting one type of fish for another you should try to use a fish with the same texture and a similiar taste. For example, if you want to make Halibut in Mornay sauce, I would use a fish such as sole, cod, or flounder, which are low in fat and have white meat. Instead of salmon, try bluefish, which has color to its meat and a stronger fish taste due to the fat content. A good idea would be to ask the person in the fish market what fish he or she would suggest.

FOR CRAB AND SHRIMP:

KING CRAB	BLUE
DUNGENESS	TANNER
SNOW	

The crabmeat from any of these are basically the same in flavor and texture. When cooked and picked from their shells, any of these may be substituted for each other.

In some recipes, you may interchange crab for shrimp, or shrimp for crab—that's where you become creative. For example, make Shrimp Cakes instead of Crab Cakes by using one cup cooked and peeled shrimp meat (coarsely chopped, about the size of peas) instead of crabmeat. Or make a shrimp-filled avocado by substituting the same amount of crabmeat with cooked, peeled, and coarsely chopped shrimp meat. Fish may also be used in place of shrimp or crab, however, I suggest a white meat fish, such as halibut, sole, or whitefish, since they would be most similar to the shellfish as they are low in fat and white in color.

When substituting combinations of seafood, again, use seafood with the same texture and taste. For example, the recipe for Seafood Fettucine calls for one cup small peeled shrimp and one cup sea scallops cut into bit-size pieces. You could use crab in place of shrimp and a fish such as halibut in place of scallops. Just use your imagination and favorite seafood.

BASIC WAYS TO COOK SEAFOOD

DEEP-FRYING

For breaded or battered fish, place the pieces in a deep-fryer wire basket and slowly lower into heated oil (375°F). Fry for three to five minutes, until the pieces are golden brown and floating. This method is great for fried clams or beer-battered halibut. Anything that is battered turns out golden brown.

BROILING

In an oven, place a rack about five inches below the heat source. Place the fish skin side down and allow to cook for five minutes per inch, per side. Baste during cooking with butter or melted fat.

POACHING

The least greasy method for cooking fish is poaching. When a recipe calls for one cup of fish meat, such as salmon or halibut, I would buy a fillet since it has the least amount of bones. Wrap the fish in cheese-cloth to keep it from flaking apart during cooking. Then, in a fish poacher or a shallow pan, bring enough water to cover the fish to a boil over high heat with a dash of salt. Add the fish, reduce the heat to simmer, and cook for four to six minutes per pound for a fillet or steak. When finished cooking, strain and let cool on a plate. Drain on paper towels. Then peel off and discard any skin, pull out any visible bones with your fingers and carefully flake the meat with your fingers, feeling for smaller bones. You are now ready to use the fish for any recipe you like. Poaching keeps fish moist and is the best cooking method for watching calories.

BAKING

Place a cleaned, dressed fish in a lightly greased baking dish. Baste with oil or butter during cooking to keep moist, at approximately 350°F, until the fish flakes easily with a knife. This works well when you want to brown the fish slightly or if you are browning a sauce or bread crumbs on top of the fish.

STEAMING

Place a wire rack or basket into a deep pot with a tight cover. Fill the pot with approximately three inches of water and bring to a full boil. Cover tightly with a lid and steam the fish for five to eight minutes per pound. When fish is placed in a pot it should be kept above the water by the basket or rack. Remember to add more boiling water every now and then, in case the water evaporates.

PAN-FRYING

Dip a clean, dressed small fish or fish fillets in milk or eggs and then into bread crumbs, cornmeal, or flour. Heat a half-inch of oil in a pan. Place the fish in the hot oil in a single layer and cook for about two minutes per side, turning fish over once halfway through cooking.

BROILED SALMON STEAKS

SPICY GRILLED SALMON STEAKS

ORIENTAL SALMON BARBECUE

POACHED SALMON WITH ORANGE SAUCE

WHOLE SALMON STUFFED WITH WILD RICE

ALASKAN SALMON DENALI

SCANDINAVIAN SALMON

COLD SALMON WITH ASPIC

SALMON FILLET EN CROUTE

SALMON WITH BACON BATTER

CHILLED SALMON MOUSSE

SWEDISH SALMON PUDDING

SALMON WITH PASTA

SALMON ON ASPARAGUS WITH HOLLANDAISE

SALMON WITH WHITE WINE SAUCE

BAKED SALMON WITH VEGETABLES

SALMON GRILLED IN FOIL

SALMON WITH PARMESAN-FENNEL BUTTER

BROILED SALMON STEAKS

Broiling salmon steaks is a quick and easy way to prepare this flavorful fish. It is also good if you are counting calories: One 4-ounce broiled steak with butter has only 201 calories.

Sauces such as meunière (lemon butter), wine, dill, or just plain fresh lemon juice go well with broiled salmon. This salmon is nice served with asparagus spears and a small garnish of lemon wedges, which can be used on both the salmon as well as the asparagus.

SERVES 6

6   1½"-thick-salmon steaks
½   cup butter

Preheat over to 550°F (Broil). Place oven rack on topmost notch.

Melt the butter in a small saucepan. Lightly grease a broiler pan with 1 or 2 tablespoons of the melted butter.

Place salmon steaks on broiler pan and, using a basting brush (or spoon if you don't have a brush), lightly paint the top of salmon with butter.

Place on top rack in oven for approximately 7 minutes on each side. Baste with more butter after turning steaks, and once again after they are out of the oven. Serve.

SPICY GRILLED SALMON STEAKS

When barbecuing, most people think of hamburgers and hot dogs. However, salmon is very easy to barbecue, as well as delicious and a change of pace. You will need a grill for this recipe.

SERVES 6

6   1½"–2"-thick salmon
    steaks

SPICY SAUCE

½	cup ketchup	¼	cup Worcestershire sauce
½	cup honey	1	teaspoon chili powder
1	medium onion, minced		Pinch cayenne pepper
¼	cup Dijon mustard	1	teaspoon lemon juice

Lightly grease and preheat barbecue grill.

In a large mixing bowl combine sauce ingredients until well blended.

Place salmon steaks on grill. Brush with some sauce. Grill for 5 to 7 minutes, turn. Brush other side of fish and cook for another 5 to 7 minutes. Watch the fish carefully when cooking to make sure the steaks do not overcook, becoming dry and flaky.

Before serving, heat remaining sauce over low heat. Serve with salmon, either over steaks or on the side.

ORIENTAL SALMON BARBECUE

This recipe has an Oriental flavor and is nice to serve with fresh-cut pieces of pineapple. You'll need a barbecue grill.

SERVES 6

ORIENTAL SAUCE

½   cup soy sauce
¼   cup brown sugar
1   tablespoon grated *¼ tsp powdered*
      gingerroot
2   cloves garlic, pressed or *¼ tsp powdered*
      minced
2   tablespoons sesame oil

6   ½"-thick salmon steaks

Lightly grease grill and heat.

GARNISH

Lemon wedges
Parsley sprigs

Try again — a little strong perhaps ✓

In a large ceramic bowl thoroughly mix sauce ingredients. Place salmon steaks on large platter and pour sauce over them; let sit for 15 minutes before grilling. Place salmon steaks on grill and cook for 3 to 5 minutes per side over medium-hot coals.

Remove from grill and serve with lemon wedges and parsley sprigs.

6 # 6:30 in microwave for 3/4 lb — 2 servings

POACHED SALMON WITH ORANGE SAUCE

This recipe calls for a poached salmon fillet; however, you can broil 6 individual salmon steaks (1½" thick) or a 3-pound salmon fillet if you'd prefer. (See recipe for Broiled Salmon Steaks, page 28.) Prepare the sauce while the salmon fillets are cooking so that the sauce is ready when the fish is.

SERVES 6

3   cups Fish Stock (page 178) or chicken or vegetable broth may be substituted)
1   3-pound salmon fillet, or 6 1½"-thick salmon steaks

GARNISH

Orange slices
Watercress

ORANGE SAUCE

3   tablespoons butter
¼   cup flour
½   teaspoon ginger powder
    Pinch dry mustard
¼   cup orange juice
⅓   cup Cointreau (an orange liqueur)
2   tablespoons grated orange peel

In a fish poacher (see sidebar) or saucepan heat fish stock over medium heat to a low boil. Add salmon fillet and simmer for 10 to 15 minutes, until flesh is firm.

Meanwhile, make the sauce. In a saucepan melt the butter over medium heat. Add flour, ginger, and mustard. Slowly stir in juice, Cointreau, and orange peel. Stir until slightly thickened (to a creamy soup consistency). Cover and keep sauce warm over very low heat, stirring frequently, while salmon is cooking so that sauce does not stick to pan and burn.

Remove and drain salmon by placing on a plate, with paper towels underneath the fish.

Place on warm platter and top salmon with orange sauce, or pour sauce into bottom of a serving platter and place salmon on top. Garnish with orange slices and watercress, then serve.

FISH POACHING

Using a fish poacher is the perfect way to poach fish—the oblong-shape pan is the right size for fish or a fish fillet. The poacher has a perforated rack inside so that the fish is not on the bottom of the pan, and therefore not on direct heat from the stove. Before poaching fish, wrap in cheesecloth leaving extra material on both ends to use as handles. This helps the fish to keep its shape during cooking and when being handled.

Fill the poacher with water so that the fish is covered with liquid. Bring water to a boil and place the fish inside on top of the rack. Cover and cook for 5 to 7 minutes per pound over medium-high heat. When done, place on a platter lined with paper towels to drain.

If you do not have a fish poacher you can use a nonstick skillet. Fill three-quarters full with water, bring to a boil, and carefully place fish in the pan. Cook for the same amount of time as in a poacher and remove with a slotted spoon.

If you would like to steam a fish in a fish poacher, simply add less water so that the water comes up to the fish rack but does not cover the fish.

WHOLE SALMON STUFFED WITH WILD RICE

This is a great dinner to serve when entertaining because most of the work may be done in advance, and it looks very impressive when served.

SERVES 6

1	4–5-pound silver or red salmon, dressed (cleaned, leaving the head on)	¼	cup butter
		½	cup chopped scallions
		½	cup sliced mushroom caps
		¼	cup minced parsley
3	tablespoons vegetable oil	⅓	cup finely chopped celery
2	teaspoons salt		
	4–6 ounces uncooked wild rice		

GARNISH

Spinach leaves or
watercress
lemon wedges

Wash the dressed salmon. Rub inside and out with vegetable oil and salt. Set aside.

Prepare the wild rice according to the directions on the package. If no directions, rinse rice and add to 4 cups boiling water, reduce heat, and simmer, covered, for 30 to 40 minutes.

Preheat oven to 350°F. Lightly grease an oblong baking pan.

In a saucepan melt butter and sauté scallions, mushrooms, parsley, and celery over low heat until the mushrooms absorb the butter. Add to the wild rice and mix well.

Stuff the inside of the salmon with the wild rice mixture. Stitch the fish closed, or use toothpicks to close the belly loosely . If you stitch, use cooking string (you can get string from your butcher or cooking store). Pierce small holes in the fish with a knife, and stitch string through the holes.

Place salmon in baking pan and bake for 40 to 45 minutes, until the fish is done (firm flesh and flaky meat).

On a large platter make a bed of fresh spinach leaves or watercress, then place the salmon on top. Add lemon wedges in a decorative pattern around the edges of the platter. Serve.

ALASKAN SALMON DENALI

The following recipe has been donated by Mark Linden, chef of Josephine's Restaurant, located at the top of the Sheraton Anchorage Hotel. I suggest making the sauce first and keeping it warm until the salmon is cooked.

SERVES 4

GINGER-LIME SAUCE

1	cup white wine	4	cups cream
3	shallots, minced	2	tablespoons cornstarch mixed with enough water to make a paste
3	white peppercorns, cracked (in a garlic press or mortar)		Dash salt and pepper
1	lime, peeled and diced, peel reserved	3	cups Court Bouillon (page 179)
1	small gingerroot	4	6-ounce salmon fillets
2	tablespoons sugar		

GARNISH

Julienne of lime peel
Lemon slices
Parsley sprigs

Add wine, shallots, peppercorns, lime, ginger, and sugar to a small pot and cook over medium heat. Allow to reduce in volume by one-half. Add cream and allow to come to a boil, then simmer gently for 20 minutes. Stir cornstarch mixture into sauce over low heat and continue to stir for 3 to 5 minutes, until sauce is a mud-thick consistency. Add salt and pepper. Strain sauce through a sieve. Keep warm until ready to serve over salmon.

In a fish poacher (see page 32) or saucepan heat court bouillon over high heat until boiling. Add salmon fillets, place a lid over the pan, and simmer for 10 to 15 minutes, or until flesh is firm. Remove salmon and drain well.

Place fish on a warm platter and cover with ginger-lime sauce. Garnish with lime peels, lemon, and parsley.

SCANDINAVIAN SALMON

ince the fish is served chilled, this recipe makes an excellent dinner or lunch on a hot day.

SERVES 6

2–3	quarts water
¼	cup lemon juice
3	tablespoons salt
2	teaspoons vegetable oil
1	2½-pound salmon roast

SAUCE   GARNISH

1	cup sour cream	Lettuce
2	teaspoons horseradish	Watercress
1	teaspoon sugar	Cucumbers, sliced
3	tablespoons chopped chives	Parsley sprigs

In a fish poacher (page 32) or saucepan bring water, lemon juice, salt, and oil to a boil.

For easy handling of fish to and from the poacher, wrap in cheesecloth leaving enough material at the end to use as handles when transferring fish to and from the pot. Cook fish for 7 to 8 minutes per pound—17 to 20 minutes—over simmering water.

Remove fish, drain on platter with paper towels under, and let cool to room temperature. Then cover with plastic wrap and chill in the refrigerator.

In a cup or small bowl blend together sauce ingredients.

When ready to serve fish, peel skin from salmon and carefully separate fish meat from bones using a fork. Place fish fillet on platter and top with sauce. Garnish with greens, such as lettuce, watercress, sliced cucumbers, and parsley. Serve.

COLD SALMON WITH ASPIC

In many foreign countries one of the favorite ways of serving salmon is chilled. Decorative vegetables such as thin-sliced cucumbers, watercress leaves, and dill placed on the fish before the glaze gives a beautiful appearance when served. It is a good idea to cook the salmon the day before so that it is thoroughly chilled when working with the aspic glaze.

SERVES 6

1   3½–4-pound whole salmon, cleaned, with head still attached

ASPIC

2   cups bouillon
2   tablespoons gelatin

GARNISH

Lettuce leaves or watercress
Cherry tomatoes
Lemon slices
Scallions, chopped

Follow recipe for bouillon, under Soups and Chowders.

Reserve 2 cups bouillon. Pour rest into a fish poacher (see page 32) or an oblong pan long enough to poach one whole salmon.

Rinse whole salmon. Wrap in cheesecloth with ends of cloth cut long enough to use as handles when moving the fish.

Bring all bouillon, except 2 cups reserved for the aspic, to a boil, and carefully place salmon in the pan. Reduce heat to low and cover. Cook salmon for about 8 minutes per pound of fish, 28 to 32 minutes.

When salmon is done, remove carefully by holding cheesecloth ends and lifting it to a large serving platter. Carefully, going against the grain, remove skin and any gray-colored meat (which is fat), leaving a nice pink surface. Cover with plastic wrap and place salmon in the refrigerator until thoroughly chilled—3 to 5 hours or overnight.

While salmon chills, make aspic. When working with aspic, make sure that everything, even your utensils, is chilled. Pour 1½ cups of reserved bouillon into a mixing bowl and bring remaining ½ cup to a boil. Dissolve gelatin in hot bouillon. When completely dissolved, pour into a mixing bowl with the other 1½ cups. Stir well. Place in the refrigerator until it starts to set (about 1 hour).

Meanwhile decorate salmon with vegetables, using any vegetables you like, such as thin-sliced cucumber sprinkled with dill, watercress leaves, or the meat of the tomato for some bright red color.

Start pouring aspic over thoroughly chilled fish by using a large spoon and applying in thin coats. Chill salmon in between coats. Spoon up drippings of aspic that run off fish to reuse in next coat. (A suggestion: Place salmon carefully on a wire rack over a large pan so that excess aspic drips into pan below and can be easily reused.) Continue this process until you have used all aspic liquid or have achieved desired thickness of aspic glaze you like.

The beautiful salmon is now ready to serve! Garnish by framing with lettuce leaves and cherry tomatoes, lemons, and chopped scallions sprinkled on top to enhance the appearance.

VARIATION: Using the same recipe and ingredients as above, substitute six 4-ounce salmon steaks for the whole salmon. Individually wrap the steaks in cheesecloth and poach in boiling bouillon, preferably in a poaching pan. If you don't have a poaching pan, use a saucepan. Set the steaks on the poaching rack so that the water covers the steaks when boiling, or if using saucepan, make sure water covers steaks. For an average 1-inch steak, the cooking time will be 4 to 5 minutes. Proceed as above.

SERVING SUGGESTION: This beautiful salmon goes well served with sliced cucumbers marinated in white vinegar and sprinkled with dillweed. Also low in calories, the whole meal, using 4-ounce steaks and ½ cup cucumbers, is only about 200 calories per serving.

SALMON FILLET EN CROUTE

I f you ever need an elegant recipe, this one is perfect. I suggest making the pastry shell first, so that it is ready when you need it. The pastry dough may also be made in advance; chill, covered, until ready to use. Or a frozen pastry shell may be substituted for the dough.

I suggest serving asparagus and a nice salad of seasonal greens with this dish to complete an excellent classic dinner.

SERVES 8

PASTRY SHELL

1⅓   cups all-purpose flour
½   cup butter (cold)
2–3 tablespoons cold white
       wine or water
1   egg yolk

SALMON

2   tablespoons butter
1   1½-pound salmon fillet
       Approximately 2 cups
         white wine

SAUCE

½   cup milk
2   tablespoons butter
3   shallots, minced
¼   cup chopped mushrooms
2   tablespoons white wine
2   tablespoons flour
½   cup sour cream
2   eggs, hard-boiled and
       chopped

Preheat oven to 400°F. Grease and flour a cookie sheet.

Put flour in a large mixing bowl and cut in butter until mixture resembles coarse meal, or small peas. Add wine or water and egg yolk and mix thoroughly. Divide dough in half. Roll out dough into an oblong shape, large enough to hold the fillet, and place on cookie sheet. Cover cookie sheet and the last half of dough with plastic wrap so that it will not become dry.

In a large saucepan melt 2 tablespoons butter over low heat. Add salmon and cook for 3 minutes on each side. Add enough wine to cover salmon—approximately 2 cups—raise heat to medium-high, cover, bring to a simmer, and cook for 6 to 8 minutes. Remove from heat and let salmon cool in its poaching liquid.

In a small saucepan scald milk by stirring constantly over medium heat, bringing the milk almost to a boil, then remove from heat and cool in a separate container.

In a skillet, melt 2 tablespoons butter and sauté shallots until soft. Add mushrooms, 2 tablespoons white wine, and the scalded milk. Heat slowly.

In a separate small bowl mix flour, sour cream, and hard-boiled eggs. When milk mixture is almost at a boil, slowly add sour cream mixture with a whisk. Stir over medium-high heat for approximately 3 minutes, until it thickens to a puddinglike stage. Set aside.

Roll out the remaining dough into another oblong shape that is large enough to encase fillet.

Spoon a thin layer of sauce on bottom of pastry shell. Place fish on top of it and roll up edges of fish so that when topped with sauce the sauce doesn't run out. Pour remaining sauce over fish. Place remaining dough over top of fish and press edges together with a fork or with your fingers to seal fish and sauce inside.

Bake for 20 to 25 minutes, until the pastry is a golden brown. Serve.

NOTE: If you desire a shiny crust, brush the outer pastry with a well-beaten egg.

SALMON WITH BACON BATTER

If you have a food processor, it will help you make a delicate batter for this recipe with less effort. If you don't have one, make sure you mince the bacon well by hand. Also, be sure to drain the bacon on paper towels to remove excess grease before mincing.

SERVES 6

BACON BATTER

½ cup minced cooked bacon	1 2–2¼-pound salmon
½ cup milk	fillet, cut into desired
½ cup fresh bread crumbs	serving sizes (not more
1 whole egg plus 1 egg yolk	than 1″-thick cubes)
¼ teaspoon dried thyme	Approximately 2 cups
½ teaspoon garlic powder	vegetable oil
Dash salt and pepper	Lemon wedges

In a saucepan bring bacon and milk to a boil over medium heat, stirring. Continue to stir and let mixture gently simmer for 2 to 3 minutes. Set aside to cool.

In a food processor or blender add remaining ingredients and blend. Add cooled milk and bacon to dry mixture, then blend until a mud-thick paste results. You may need to add either more crumbs or milk to get the desired result.

Pat salmon dry.

In a deep fryer heat oil in 375°F. If you don't have a deep fryer, heat oil in a heavy skillet over medium-high heat. To test if the oil is hot enough, lightly sprinkle water into oil by wetting your hands and flicking your fingers over—but not close—to oil. If oil spatters and lightly bubbles, it is ready. When hot, dip a piece of salmon in batter, letting excess drip off, and fry until a golden brown—about 4 minutes, depending on size of salmon pieces. Be careful when working with hot oil since it tends to spatter. (If you have children, keep them away from where you are working.) Continue this process until all of the salmon pieces are done.

Serve with lemon wedges and ENJOY!

SERVING SUGGESTION: A good and easy-to-make accompaniment is individual cups of sour cream with sprinkles of paprika on top.

CHILLED SALMON MOUSSE

This is a very elegant and different way to serve salmon. It is especially nice when molded in a fish mold and served on a large platter and decoratively garnished. It can be served as an appetizer or as a main course.

SERVES 8

2	envelopes unflavored gelatin	3	dashes Tabasco sauce
½	cup boiling water	½	teaspoon paprika
¼	cup cold water	1	teaspoon parsley flakes
½	cup mayonnaise	1	teaspoon salt
	Juice from ½ lemon	1	pound cooked, drained, and flaked salmon meat
1	scallion, chopped	½	cup heavy cream, whipped

Lightly oil a mold.

In a bowl mix the gelatin with the boiling water and stir until dissolved, then add the cold water.

In a separate bowl mix mayonnaise, lemon juice, scallions, Tabasco, paprika, parsley, and salt. When gelatin mixture has cooled to room temperature, mix together with mayonnaise mixture. Chill until it is just starting to gel. At this point, add salmon. Lightly fold in whipped cream.

Pour mousse into mold and chill until firmly set, about 3 hours.

Transfer to a serving platter, unmold, and serve as is, or with a nice dill, lemon, or white sauce (see Chapter 10, "Sauces and Dips").

MOLDS

Usually, any type of aluminum or tin gelatin mold will work when making a seafood mousse. However, a Teflon-lined mold works better when you are trying to unmold the mousse—it does not have a tendency to stick as much as one without Teflon.

Place the mousse in a lightly greased mold. When ready to serve, place a large platter over the top of the mold and turn upside down so that the mold is upside down on the serving platter. You may tap the outside of the mold gently with a spoon to help the mousse fall.

SWEDISH SALMON PUDDING

I find this recipe makes a great appetizer served on a bed of lettuce with toast points, capers, and diced onions.

SERVES 2–3

2	cups cooked, drained, and flaked salmon meat	¼	cup butter, softened
1	teaspoon salt	2	cups cream
¼	teaspoon white pepper	2	eggs
1	teaspoon grated nutmeg		Parsley or dill sprigs

Preheat oven to 325°F. Grease a plain deep, round mold or casserole dish well.

Put salmon, salt, pepper, and nutmeg in a large mixing bowl. Add softened butter and beat with an electric mixer. When butter is blended with salmon, slowly add cream and eggs, then continue to beat for approximately 2 to 4 minutes, until mixture is smooth.

Put mixture in the mold or casserole dish. Set dish in a large pan of hot water (enough water in the pan to come at least halfway up to top of dish). Bake for 1 to 1½ hours, or until a knife inserted in center comes out clean.

Serve steaming hot with parsley or dill springs as garnish.

SALMON WITH PASTA

I f you garnish this dish with 2 tablespoons chopped parsley and ¼ cup salmon roe caviar, you will have a festive-looking meal that is easy to make.

SERVES 4

1   cup butter
1   small onion, minced
1   clove garlic, pressed (using a garlic press)
¼   cup white wine
½   cup Fish Stock (page 178)
2   tablespoons minced fresh parsley
1   pound salmon, skinned and boned, cut into bite-size cubes
1   1-pound package dried or fresh thin spaghetti
     Grated Parmesan cheese

In a large skillet melt butter over low heat, being careful not to burn it. Add onion and garlic and sauté until onion is translucent.

Add wine, stock, and parsley. Bring to a boil and then add salmon and reduce heat to a simmer for 8 to 10 minutes.

In a pot of boiling water cook pasta according to package instructions. Drain well and place on a large serving platter. Pour salmon mixture over top and toss lightly. Sprinkle grated Parmesan cheese over top and serve.

SALMON ON ASPARAGUS WITH HOLLANDAISE

Since timing is very important (you're cooking salmon fillets, asparagus and making sauce, all to be served at the same time) it makes things much easier to be well organized in this recipe. Cut and steam the asparagus ahead of time and place in vegetable steamer. Have your bread crumbs and beaten eggs placed in shallow dishes and your sauce ingredients out and ready to use. This dish is well worth the effort!

SERVES 4

2 cups fine dry bread crumbs	1 recipe Hollandaise Sauce,
4 eggs, well beaten	heated (page 164)
4 10-ounce salmon fillets	Parsley sprigs
¾ cup butter	
1 pound (approximately 20 average-size) asparagus spears	

In 2 shallow dishes place bread crumbs and eggs. Dip salmon fillet in eggs, then dredge in bread crumbs. Place fillets aside on a plate lined with paper towels while you melt ¼ cup butter over medium-low heat in a sauté pan. Add fillets and cook for approximately 10 minutes on each side. When salmon is finished cooking, remove from heat and let sit in pan.

While salmon is cooking, steam asparagus spears in a vegetable steamer for 5 to 10 minutes, then drain. In a skillet melt ½ cup butter then add asparagus spears. Turn off heat and let asparagus sit while you make hollandaise.

When finished, heat asparagus and salmon for 1 minute over medium heat. Transfer approximately 5 spears of asparagus onto individually heated plates. Place salmon fillets on asparagus and then top with hollandaise. Serve immediately, topped with parsley sprigs for garnish.

SALMON WITH WHITE WINE SAUCE

This recipe is not only delicious but simple to make. You can serve broccoli or asparagus with the salmon, also topped with wine sauce.

SERVES 6

6	6-ounce salmon fillets	1	cup cream
½	cup butter	2	teaspoons flour mixed with
1	cup white wine		1 tablespoon water
2	cups clam juice		Capers

Preheat oven to 350°F.

Pat fillets dry. Melt butter in a shallow 13″- × -9″ baking pan.

Coat fish in butter and arrange in pan. Pour wine over fish. Bake for 10 minutes, basting frequently with pan juices. Transfer fish to heated plate or platter and keep warm.

Pour broth from baking pan into a saucepan, add clam juice, and boil for 10 minutes. Add cream and boil rapidly for another 10 minutes to reduce liquid. Whisk flour paste into broth mixture and cook until thickened.

Pour sauce on the bottom of a platter, placing fish on top. Sprinkle capers on salmon for garnish.

BAKED SALMON WITH VEGETABLES

Not only is this recipe simple and healthy, it's also low in calories. A nice way to serve the salmon is on a bed of rice, with the vegetables on top.

SERVES 6

¼ cup olive oil
6   ½-pound salmon steaks, or
      1 3-pound fillet
     Salt and pepper
1   medium tomato, diced
1   small zucchini, diced

¼ cup minced onion
⅓ cup minced green pepper
2   tablespoons fresh parsley
2   tablespoons pressed garlic
     Juice from 1 lemon
¼ cup butter, melted

Preheat oven to 350°F. Grease a shallow baking dish with olive oil.

Season salmon to taste with salt and pepper. Arrange in one layer in baking dish.

Combine vegetables, parsley, and garlic, then spoon over fish. Drizzle lemon juice and butter over top and cover with tin foil. Bake for about 30 minutes, or until fish flakes easily with a fork. Serve.

SALMON GRILLED IN FOIL

This is a great dinner not only because it tastes so good, but because there are no dishes that have to be cleaned! You will need a barbecue grill.

SERVES 4

1	2-pound salmon fillet		Juice from ½ lemon
1	stick (½ cup) butter	¼	cup grated Parmesan
1	large tomato, diced		cheese
2	scallions, chopped	¼	cup dry white wine

Heat barbecue grill.

Lightly grease a sheet of aluminum foil with butter and place salmon fillet on top. Slice a stick of butter into approximately 12 pats and place on salmon. Sprinkle remaining ingredients on top. Wrap in foil and grill for 12 to 15 minutes. Transfer onto warm platter and serve.

⅓ recipe minus cheese on 1 trout
wrap - bake in 350° 1 hour. OK

SALMON WITH PARMESAN-FENNEL BUTTER

If you are a fennel fan like I am, you'll love this.

SERVES 4

¼ cup butter
1 tablespoon lightly crushed
    fennel seeds
  Juice from ½ lemon

¼ cup white wine
1 2-pound salmon fillet
¼ cup grated Parmesan
    cheese

In a large skillet melt butter over low heat. Add fennel seeds, lemon juice, and white wine. Raise heat to medium and add salmon fillet, cover, and let simmer for 8 to 10 minutes.

Sprinkle fillet with Parmesan cheese and cover for another minute. Remove from heat and serve.

CHAPTER

3

HALIBUT

POACHED HALIBUT WITH SHRIMP SAUCE

BROILED HALIBUT STEAKS

BEER-BATTERED HALIBUT

BAKED HALIBUT CHEEKS IN MORNAY SAUCE

HALIBUT FILLET WITH GINGER SAUCE

HALIBUT CHEEKS MARINARA

SWEET AND SOUR HALIBUT

HALIBUT KEBOBS

HALIBUT CREPES

GRILLED HALIBUT IN FOIL

SAUTÉED HALIBUT

SPANISH HALIBUT

CALIFORNIA HALIBUT

FENNEL-TOMATO HALIBUT

HALIBUT WITH CREOLE STUFFING

GRILLED MARINATED HALIBUT

HALIBUT IN VEGETABLE-WINE SAUCE

POACHED HALIBUT WITH SHRIMP SAUCE

This creamy yet light shrimp sauce, when spooned over halibut, instantly turns your fish into a gastronomic delight.

SHRIMP SAUCE

¼ cup butter	¼ teaspoon salt
1 tablespoon finely chopped onion	¼ teaspoon freshly ground white pepper
Approximately ¾ pound medium raw shrimp, peeled, trimmed, minced (page 123)	Approximately ¼ cup sherry, or to taste
	1 2-pound halibut fillet
3 tablespoons tomato paste	½ teaspoon salt
2 cups light cream	Watercress

In a skillet melt butter and sauté onion for 2 minutes over medium heat. Add minced shrimp meat and sauté for 2 more minutes. Transfer mixture to food processor and add remaining ingredients. Blend.

When well blended, return to low heat and simmer until thickened, stirring constantly until you have a creamy, mud-thick texture. Turn off heat and cover sauce while poaching halibut.

Fill fish poacher (see page 32) with water. Bring to a boil with salt. When water is boiling, place halibut fillet on rack and cook for approximately 14 minutes (5 to 7 minutes per pound). Fish will be done when no longer translucent in center and meat flakes easily with fork.

With a spatula, transfer fillet onto a large warm serving platter, blot any excess liquid on fish and platter with paper towel. Top with shrimp sauce and garnish with watercress around platter, with one sprig on top of fish.

BROILED HALIBUT STEAKS

Preparing broiled halibut steaks is a little different than broiling most other kinds of seafood steaks. Halibut is low in fat content and tends to get dry and flaky if not basted or if overcooked.

SERVES 6

2   tablespoons vegetable oil
6   1½″-thick halibut steaks
¼   cup butter, melted

GARNISH

Lemon wedges
Parsley sprigs

Preheat oven to 550°F (Broil). Coat broiling pan with vegetable oil.

Place halibut steaks on broiling pan. Brush halibut with melted butter (a spoon if you don't have a brush), until top of halibut is lightly coated.

Place halibut on top oven rack. Cook fish for approximately 7 minutes per side. Baste with melted butter after turning steaks, and once again when out of oven. Garnish with lemon wedges and parsley. Serve.

BEER-BATTERED HALIBUT

This probably is the most popular Alaskan recipe for halibut. It also works well with shrimp and scallops. My favorite way to serve this meal is with bowls of Cocktail Sauce and/or Tartar Sauce (see Chapter 10, "Sauces and Dips"), lemon wedges, or other tasty dishes scattered about the table.

SERVES 4

BEER BATTER

3	eggs		Vegetable oil
1	cup beer	1	2-pound halibut fillet, cut
1	tablespoon vegetable oil		into bite-size chunks
1	teaspoon salt		
2	cups flour		

Crack eggs and separate, putting the whites into a small dish; refrigerate. Put yolks into a large mixing bowl. Add beer, 1 tablespoon oil, salt, and 1 cup flour. Mix well.

Take egg whites out of the refrigerator and whip them until stiff, then carefully fold them into batter.

Heat deep fryer to 375°F. If you don't have a deep fryer, heat 1½ cups vegetable oil over medium-high heat in a deep saucepan. You must be very careful when working with hot oil. (Make sure little children aren't near you.) To test if oil is hot enough, lightly sprinkle water into oil by wetting your hands and flicking your fingers over— but not close to—oil, so that it doesn't spatter on you. If oil spatters and lightly bubbles, it is ready.

Coat halibut in remaining 1 cup flour, dip in beer batter, and fry (only a few pieces at a time) until golden brown, 4 to 5 minutes. Drain on paper towels. Serve.

BAKED HALIBUT CHEEKS IN MORNAY SAUCE

Although often neglected, halibut cheeks come from the jaw of the halibut, and in my opinion are the best part of the fish. They vary in size and have a texture close to that of scallops because of the direction of the grain. They are difficult to find in stores because of the work involved in removing the cheek from the rest of the fish. Many people don't bother to remove the boneless cheeks, but once you taste them, I'm sure you'll agree it's worth the extra effort.

SERVES 6–8

3   pounds halibut cheeks
1   recipe Mornay Sauce (page
      165)
1   tomato, sliced
½   cup grated Swiss cheese
     Paprika

Preheat oven to 350°F. Lightly butter a casserole dish.

Arrange halibut cheeks in casserole dish and pour sauce over top. Bake for 30 minutes.

Place a layer of sliced tomato and grated Swiss cheese over top. Turn heat up to 550°F and broil, uncovered, for 7 to 10 minutes, until golden brown on top. Sprinkle with paprika and serve.

HALIBUT FILLET WITH GINGER SAUCE

This is one of my favorite ways to cook halibut: It's very simple and keeps the fish moist due to the poaching. Ginger is native to the West Indies, and its most common use is to season food. However, the Chinese would often add ginger to tea as a home remedy for stomach aches. Americans use ginger for its spicy unique flavoring.

SERVES 4

4   ½-pound halibut fillets

GARNISH

Thin lemon slices
Watercress sprigs

GINGER SAUCE

2   tablespoons plus 1 teaspoon sesame oil
1   tablespoon butter
2   tablespoons minced fresh mushroom caps
1   fresh gingerroot, pared and julienned (enough to fill ¼ cup)
2   scallions, white and green parts, chopped
1   tablespoon soy sauce
1   teaspoon sugar
2   tablespoons sherry (optional)

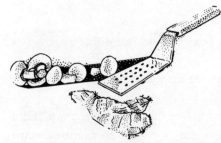

Rinse fillets in cold water, pat dry, and coat in sesame oil. (In order not to rinse off the flavoring of the sesame oil, steam the fillets in a fish poacher [see page 32] or in an oblong pan filled with water to where the rack sits.) Cover and cook for 12 to 15 minutes, depending on the thickness, until fish is white in middle of fillet—*not* transparent —and flakes easily.

Meanwhile, in a small saucepan melt butter. Add mushrooms, ginger, and scallions. Sauté until soft, then add soy sauce, sugar, and sherry.

Take halibut out of the poacher and arrange on a serving platter. Pat fillets with paper towels to remove excess liquid then pour ginger sauce over fillets. Garnish with thin lemon slices and watercress sprigs for a nice finishing touch. Serve immediately.

HALIBUT CHEEKS MARINARA

Halibut served with this tomato sauce works well with garlic bread and salad. It's a nice, different alternative to pasta and marinara sauce.

SERVES 4

¼   cup olive oil
 2   cloves garlic, minced
 2   medium onions, sliced
 4   large ripe tomatoes,
       peeled and seeded,
       then chopped
¼   cup chopped fresh
       mushrooms
¼   cup green pepper,
       chopped
 1   8-ounce can whole peeled
       tomatoes, drained,
       seeded, and coarsely
       chopped
 2   pounds halibut cheeks
       (the larger the better)

GARNISH

Parsley sprigs
Lemon wedges

In a large heavy pan heat oil and sauté garlic and onion until soft. Add tomatoes, mushrooms, and green pepper. Simmer over medium heat for 5 minutes, stirring frequently. Then add canned tomatoes. Add halibut cheeks and simmer for another 15 minutes, covered.

Transfer to a large warm platter, garnish with parsley and lemon, and serve.

PEELING AND SEEDING TOMATOES

Fill a deep pot half full of water, and bring to a boil. Place tomato on slotted spoon and dip in boiling water for *1 minute*. Remove tomato and dip in cold water, then peel skin. On a cutting board, slice tomatoes in quarters and remove seeds.

SWEET AND SOUR HALIBUT

Everybody loves the old Chinese traditional sweet and sour pork. Halibut, with its juicy white meat, adds a different taste to this old favorite. Even kids who are not fish fans seem to have no problem cleaning their plates. I think this dish is best when served over steamed white rice, or with the rice as a side dish.

SERVES 3

2	tablespoons flour	½	cup water	
½	teaspoon salt	1	green pepper, chopped into 1″ squares	
2	tablespoons shoyu (see note)	½	cup pineapple juice	
1	1-pound halibut fillet, cut into bite-size cubes	1	cup pineapple cubes	
¼	cup sesame oil	1	teaspoon finely chopped gingerroot	
⅓	cup sugar			
¼	cup vinegar (rice vinegar if available)			

Make a paste with flour, salt, and shoyu. Roll halibut in paste.

Heat sesame oil in a heavy skillet over medium heat. Add halibut and cook until lightly browned.

Add sugar, vinegar, water, green pepper, and pineapple juice. Simmer for 5 to 10 minutes uncovered, until halibut is thoroughly cooked. It should be white inside, not translucent, and flake easily with a fork. Add pineapple cubes and ginger. Let simmer for another 5 minutes. Serve.

NOTE: Shoyu, a powder-based Oriental seasoning, is available in Oriental or gourmet food stores, or the specialty section of supermarkets.

HALIBUT KEBOBS

You may either grill or broil halibut kebobs. My favorite method is the grill, especially if mesquite chips are used along with the charcoal. However, if you prefer to broil the fish, preheat your oven to 550°F and place your oven rack on the second notch from the top, 10 minutes before you want to cook the fish.

SERVES 4–6

MARINADE

½   cup butter
1½ teaspoons pressed garlic
      (use a garlic press)
¼   cup lemon juice
¼   cup orange juice
1   teaspoon soy sauce

2   pounds halibut fillet, cut
      into 1″ cubes
1   cup cubed zucchini
1   cup cubed papaya
1   cup cherry tomatoes

Heat grill or broiler.

In a saucepan over low heat melt butter. When butter is melted add garlic. Whisk in lemon and orange juice, and soy sauce. Remove from heat.

Add halibut and zucchini. Let marinate for 15 minutes.

Thread halibut on a skewer, alternating halibut, zucchini, papaya, and cherry tomatoes.

Broil or grill for 12 to 15 minutes, turning and basting frequently with marinade—every 4 to 5 minutes. Serve.

HALIBUT CREPES

Parts of this recipe should be made in advance—the crepe batter should be refrigerated for at least 3 hours, or overnight if possible. The crepes can be made in advance as well. (If you make the batter ahead of time, package airtight and refrigerate. It will last up to 6 days, or up to 1 month if you freeze it.) Makes approximately 12 to 18 crepes.

SERVES 6–8

CREPES

3   eggs
⅔   cup flour
1   cup milk
½   teaspoon salt
½   teaspoon curry powder

½   cup butter, softened

FILLING

1   cup white wine
1   2-pound halibut fillet
¼   cup milk
1½   cups sour cream
½   cup butter
    Approximately ½ cup
       flour
½   cup cooked, drained
       spinach
½   cup grated Parmesan
       cheese
    Paprika

In a bowl mix crepe ingredients thoroughly and then cover and refrigerate for at least 3 hours, or overnight.

In a crepe pan (a small skillet with slightly turned up edges)—5″ preferred—melt ¼ teaspoon butter. When foamy, pour in enough batter to cover bottom of pan with a thin layer, approximately ¼ cup batter, tilting pan quickly to coat entire pan surface. Cook crepe until a very light brown, flip, and slightly brown other side. Place on a piece of foil. Continue this process until batter is all gone. Cover and set crepes aside.

To make filling, heat wine in a pot large enough to hold halibut.

Gently simmer halibut, covered, for 10 minutes. Drain fish from wine over a bowl, to save the liquid. Carefully break halibut into bite-size cubes, removing any bones, skin, or fat.

In a saucepan add milk, sour cream, and 1 cup of the wine that the fish was cooked in. Add butter, then slowly add flour by sprinkling it over top and stirring. Cook sauce over medium heat until thickened to a puddinglike consistency, 6 to 8 minutes.

Preheat oven to 375°F. Lightly oil a baking dish.

Save 1 cup of sauce and put aside. Add spinach and halibut to rest of sauce, blending in the saucepan.

Fill each crepe with about ¼ cup of halibut and spinach filling, roll crepes closed. Place them in the baking dish.

Top with remaining cup of sauce and Parmesan cheese. Lightly sprinkle with paprika and bake for 8 to 10 minutes. Serve.

GRILLED HALIBUT IN FOIL

This is my favorite halibut recipe for summer cooking, especially when entertaining. It always gets rave reviews.

SERVES 4

1   stick (½ cup) lightly salted
    butter
1   2-pound halibut (fillet
    preferred but steaks may
    also be used)
    Small Bermuda onion,
    thinly sliced

1   small tomato, diced
1   tablespoon pressed garlic
½   lemon
3   tablespoons white wine
2   tablespoons grated
    Parmesan cheese

If using oven, preheat to 425°F. Otherwise, heat barbecue grill.

Take stick of butter and lightly rub over the bottom of heavy duty tin foil. Place halibut on foil. Dot halibut with sliced butter patties.

Place sliced onion, tomato, and garlic on top of fish. Squeeze juice of ½ lemon over everything, then pour wine over it. Sprinkle with Parmesan cheese.

Roll fish in the foil and place over low coals for 20 to 30 minutes (about 30 minutes in oven), until fish loses translucent color in middle and is white throughout. Serve immediately.

SAUTÉED HALIBUT

This is a simple yet classy recipe. I like to serve sautéed halibut with fresh steamed seasonal vegetables topped with butter and wild rice.

½ recipe plenty for 2 servings

SERVES 2–3

¼ cup lightly salted butter	Juice from ½ lemon, plus
3 teaspoons pressed garlic	lemon slices for garnish
2 tablespoons chopped fresh	¼ cup white wine
parsley, plus extra sprigs	1 1-pound halibut fillet
for garnish	

try ½ tsp. garlic salt

In sauté pan melt butter over medium heat and add garlic, parsley, lemon, and white wine. When all mixed, add halibut and sauté over medium-high heat until cooked thoroughly, about 3 minutes on each side.

Using one large spatula or two, carefully remove fish onto a large warm serving platter garnished with parsley sprigs and lemons—or with vegetables arranged around side of the fish. Pass the meal around the table!

SPANISH HALIBUT

This colorful dish is lovely for entertaining. You can present the fish on a large warm platter and let people take what they like. Serve with rice pilaf, tossed salad, and a pitcher of Sangria.

SERVES 6

1	3-pound halibut fillet	1	tablespoon minced fresh parsley, or 2 tablespoons dried
1	teaspoon salt		
2	tablespoons flour		
¼	cup olive oil	1	tablespoon minced fresh coriander, or ¼ teaspoon dried
2	medium onions, sliced		
½	cup white wine		
3	cloves garlic, minced		Juice from ½ lemon
1	teaspoon dried oregano	1–4	tablespoons capers
1	teaspoon mustard seeds	2	tomatoes, diced
⅛	teaspoon powdered saffron	10	black olives, slivered
		¼	cup water

Preheat oven to 350°F.

Sprinkle fish with salt and dust lightly with flour. Place in a shallow 8″-×-12″ baking dish.

Heat oil in a skillet and sauté onions until soft. Place over fish.

In a mixing bowl combine wine, garlic, oregano, mustard seeds, saffron, parsley, coriander, lemon juice, capers, tomatoes, and olives. Mix well and pour over fish.

Pour water around fish and bake uncovered for about 45 minutes. Transfer to a large warm platter and serve.

CALIFORNIA HALIBUT

This is a simple and spicy dish. You can also prepare it in advance and refrigerate until you're ready to grill.

SERVES 4

good

MARINADE

½   cup vegetable oil
½   teaspoon salt
⅛   teaspoon cayenne pepper
¼   cup fresh lemon juice
1   clove garlic, pressed
½   teaspoon powdered cumin —
    Chopped fresh parsley or
    cilantro

1   2-pound halibut fillet, cut
    into 4 pieces
Vegetable oil

might try something different

parsley would add
parsley good but use sparingly

In a small mixing bowl, combine marinade ingredients.

Place fish in glass baking dish and pour marinade over fish. Marinate for 1 hour in the refrigerator, turning fish once or twice.

Grease barbecue grill with oil, then heat.

When ready, grill fish for 4 to 5 minutes per side, or until fish flakes easily. If broiling, place fish in broiler pan on second rack from the top in the oven. Broil 5 to 7 minutes per side, basting with its juices when you turn the fish. Sprinkle with chopped parsley or fresh cilantro and serve.

OK in micro   5 min for .6 lb

FENNEL-TOMATO HALIBUT

I am a fennel and tomato fan. If you have never combined the two, I suggest you try this recipe. It's one of my all-time favorites.

SERVES 4

¼ cup butter	¼ cup white wine
1 shallot, minced	Juice of ½ lemon
4 tablespoons pressed garlic	½ teaspoon lightly crushed
1 2-pound halibut fillet,	fennel seeds
patted dry	2 tomatoes, diced

In a saucepan melt butter over medium heat, then sauté shallot and garlic until shallot is translucent. Add halibut. Increase heat to medium high, sauté halibut on both sides, approximately 2 minutes per side.

When halibut is lightly brown on each side, add white wine, lemon juice, fennel seeds, and tomatoes on sides of pan and under fish. Turn to medium heat and cook for approximately 10 minutes, slightly stirring other ingredients without moving fish.

Serve fish on platter and spoon other ingredients on top.

HALIBUT WITH CREOLE STUFFING

This is almost a complete meal in itself. Just make a salad and serve.

SERVES 5–6

CREOLE STUFFING

2	cups cooked brown rice (or brown and wild rice mixed)	3	tablespoons butter
		2	shallots, minced
⅛	teaspoon cayenne pepper	½	cup sliced mushrooms
2	tablespoons minced fresh parsley	2	thin 1-pound halibut fillets
		3	tablespoons butter
¼	cup chopped almonds		
½	cup chopped water chestnuts		

2–3 tablespoons water
Paprika

Preheat oven to 450°F. Grease a shallow baking dish with butter.

In a bowl mix rice, cayenne pepper, parsley, almonds, and water chestnuts. Set aside.

In sauté pan melt butter over medium heat, sauté shallots and mushrooms for 2 to 3 minutes. Stir in rice mixture.

In baking dish lay 1 halibut fillet in pan and spread stuffing evenly on top of fillet. Place remaining fillet on top and dot with butter. Put water on the side of the fish in the pan and bake uncovered for 25 to 35 minutes, basting fish often with its own juices.

To serve, slice into sections. Sprinkle with paprika for garnish.

GRILLED MARINATED HALIBUT

For this recipe, the marinade may be prepared ahead of time. Place fish in marinade anywhere from 30 minutes to 4 hours before you're ready to grill. The longer the fish is marinated, the more flavor it will have. The marinated mushrooms are not necessary to serve over the fish, but since they are so porous, they pick up much of the marinade flavor and are a nice accompaniment.

SERVES 8

MARINADE

½ cup soy sauce
1 cup white wine
   Juice from ½ lemon
3 tablespoons pressed garlic
3 tablespoons grated gingerroot
½ cup sesame oil (vegetable or corn oil may be substituted)
¼ cup chopped scallions

1 4-pound halibut fillet
1 pound fresh mushrooms, sliced
   vegetable oil
⅓ cup butter
2 tablespoons sesame seeds

In a bowl combine marinade ingredients. Add fish and marinate for 30 minutes to 4 hours.

Grease a barbecue grill or broiling pan with oil, and heat.

Pour off and reserve marinade.

Carefully place fish on grill over low coals and cook until fish flakes easily when tested with a fork, 10 to 15 minutes. If broiling in oven, place fillets on broiling pan and put on second rack from top. Broil for 6 to 8 minutes on each side, basting with its juices between turns.

Meanwhile, wrap mushrooms, butter, sesame seeds, and ¼ cup of leftover marinade in tin foil and place on grill. Keep on the grill until fish is ready, (10 to 15 minutes).

Serve mushrooms over fish or on the side.

SERVING SUGGESTION: This dish is great served with grilled fresh vegetables of your choice. Wrap chopped vegetables in foil with a little lemon and butter and place on grill while cooking fish and serve together.

HALIBUT IN VEGETABLE-WINE SAUCE

You may be skeptical about trying this vegetable sauce, but through the combination of the different ingredients you create a flavor that really enhances the fish. Using a food processor when grating or chopping the zucchini, carrot, and celery gives a nice uniform appearance.

SERVES 4

¼ cup olive oil	1 zucchini, grated
1 2-pound halibut fillet, cut into 2″ pieces	1 large onion, chopped
	1 large carrot, grated
1 clove garlic, pressed	2 stalks celery, chopped
1 teaspoon salt	1 large tomato, diced
Dash pepper	¼ cup water
1 tablespoon chopped fresh parsley	¾ cup white wine
	Grated Parmesan cheese
¼ cup butter	

Heat olive oil in skillet. Add halibut and sauté over medium heat until golden brown, approximately 10 minutes. Remove fish with slotted spoon to a platter and set aside.

Add garlic, salt, pepper, parsley, butter, vegetables, water, and white wine to skillet. Simmer for 10 minutes, then add halibut and cook for another 5 minutes. Top with Parmesan cheese, then serve.

4

S C A L L O P S

SCALLOPS WITH WHITE WINE AND MUSHROOMS

SIMPLE AND DELICIOUS SCALLOP SAUTÉ

PEACH SCALLOPS/ALMONDINE

BAKED SCALLOPS IN GARLIC

RED PEPPERS AND SCALLOPS IN RICE

SCALLOP FONDUE WITH MUSTARD SAUCE

SCALLOP QUENELLES WITH SHRIMP SAUCE

SCALLOPS WITH WHITE WINE AND MUSHROOMS

not real tasty – rather drippy

I've used this recipe dozens of times and always get raves. However, it is very easy to ruin this dish. I find nothing worse than to see scallops overcooked into little rubber balls. Since there are usually 10 to 15 sea scallops to a pound, they should not be cooked for more than 5 minutes. If they are much smaller, use less cooking time.

SERVES 4   *½# for 2*

1 pound scallops, rinsed, drained (see note)	1 tablespoon minced fresh parsley
2 tablespoons butter	1 clove garlic, pressed
1 medium onion, minced	1 cup dry white wine
1 pound mushrooms, caps only, thinly sliced	1 tablespoon flour
	Lemon wedges

Pat scallops dry with paper towels.

In a skillet melt butter and sauté onion, mushrooms, parsley, and garlic. When tender, add wine and flour, blending in flour well.

When just to a boil, add scallops. Cover and simmer over medium heat for 5 minutes.

Serve with lemon wedges.

NOTE: Scallops should be rinsed very quickly and lightly so as not to rinse away the flavor. Whenever a recipe calls for cooked scallops, poach scallops in simmering water 5 minutes for 1 pound of sea scallops.

5 min. OK for scallops

½ lb for 2

SIMPLE AND DELICIOUS SCALLOP SAUTÉ

good

Either bay or sea scallops may be used for this recipe. Bay scallops are usually half the size of sea scallops and therefore cannot be cooked as long.

SERVES 4

*cooked probably
5 min, not too
hot -   o k.
parsley would
add -*

1   pound scallops, quickly
      rinsed and drained
½   cup butter
3   cloves garlic, pressed
2   tablespoons grated
      Parmesan cheese
1   tablespoon minced fresh
      parsley

¼ tsp salt with margarine

Pat scallops with paper towels.

In a heavy skillet melt butter over low heat, being careful not to burn. Add garlic and scallops. Sauté for 3 to 4 minutes. Add Parmesan cheese and mix well.

Remove scallops with a slotted spoon and sprinkle with parsley.

SERVING SUGGESTION: This dish is great in the summertime, served with fresh vegetables. You can save the butter and garlic that the scallops were cooked in to drip across the top of the vegetables.

*5 min in frying pan good
for small bay scallops
marinated*

PEACH SCALLOPS ALMONDINE

This recipe calls for a fresh peach, but if peaches are out of season or unavailable, canned peaches may be substituted (drain *all* liquid).

Serve over rice pilaf (see note) and enjoy.

SERVES 3

1 pound scallops (sea scallops preferred), quickly rinsed and drained	½ teaspoon ground cardamom
2 tablespoons butter	½ teaspoon grated nutmeg
2 tablespoons slivered almonds	¼ cup sherry
1 ripe peach	2 tablespoons water
	1 teaspoon honey

Pat scallops dry with paper towels.

In a skillet melt butter over low heat. Add almonds. Keep stirring until they are lightly brown, approximately 5 minutes.

Cut a ripe peach in thick slices and then quarter slices. Add to almonds along with cardamom and nutmeg. Stir together until heated thoroughly, approximately 5 minutes. Add sherry, water, honey, and scallops.

Turn heat up to medium and bring to a boil. Reduce heat and let simmer, covered, for 3 to 5 more minutes, until scallops are done and liquid has slightly reduced.

NOTE: To make rice pilaf, instead of plain rice, substitute Fish Fumet (page 178) or chicken stock for the water called for in the recipe. Mince 2 tablespoons fresh parsley, toss into rice, and serve.

BAKED SCALLOPS IN GARLIC

This is an Italian twist on an old favorite. For those who wish to avoid the garlic, shallots may be substituted for a milder flavor.

SERVES 4

½   cup butter
3   cloves garlic, pressed, or
      2 tablespoons minced
      shallots
4   fresh mushrooms, sliced
1½ pounds scallops, quickly
      rinsed and drained
¼   cup sherry
      Dash paprika

Preheat oven to 400°F.

In a skillet melt butter with garlic or shallots over low heat and simmer for 2 to 3 minutes. Be careful not to brown butter.

In a casserole or individual dishes spread a thin, even coat of garlic butter. Add a layer of sliced mushrooms, then a layer of scallops over mushrooms. Evenly spoon rest of garlic butter over scallops. Sprinkle sherry and paprika on top. Bake for 10 to 15 minutes and serve.

RED PEPPERS AND SCALLOPS IN RICE

This recipe tastes great with brown rice. Not only is the rice unusual, it has more protein and B vitamins than white rice.

SERVES 6–8

3	cups Fish Stock (page 178) or chicken stock	4	shallots, chopped
2¼	cups white wine	1	tablespoon pressed garlic
1	pound scallops, quickly rinsed, drained, and cut into bite-size pieces	1	teaspoon dried basil
		½	teaspoon turmeric
2	cups uncooked brown rice	2	tablespoons minced fresh parsley
¼	cup olive oil		
1	red bell pepper, chopped, plus julienned slices for garnish		

In a large saucepan over high heat bring fish stock and wine to a boil. Reduce heat to medium, add scallops, cover, and poach for 3 to 5 minutes, until done.

Remove scallops with a slotted spoon and bring stock back to a boil. Add rice cover, reduce heat to medium-low, and simmer for 15 to 20 minutes, or until almost all of the liquid is absorbed.

Preheat oven to 400°F.

Meanwhile, heat oil in a heavy skillet and sauté bell pepper and shallots until shallots are translucent. Add garlic, basil, turmeric, and parsley.

When rice is done, in a medium-size bowl mix with scallops and peppers. Press firmly into a 6-cup mold, preferably a ring shape, with a nonstick or lightly oiled surface. Bake for 10 minutes.

Unmold on a large serving platter by placing serving platter on top of mold and turning upside down. Garnish with julienne slices of red bell pepper.

SCALLOP FONDUE WITH MUSTARD SAUCE

The perfect party dish—I love to enjoy this with a group of friends in front of a roaring fire after a day skiing.

SERVES 4

6	eggs, beaten
¼	cup milk
1	cup flour
¼	teaspoon salt
1½	pounds sea scallops, quickly rinsed, drained, patted dry, arranged on platter
	Mustard Sauce (see page 169)

Heat oil in fondue pot to 375°F.

In a bowl mix eggs and milk together until blended well.

In another bowl mix together flour and salt. Spear scallops, dip first into eggs, and then roll in flour.

Dip breaded scallops carefully into hot oil and cook until golden brown, approximately 1 minute.

Place mustard sauce in small bowls around the table. Dip scallops in the sauce and enjoy. (This goes well with a nice salad served on the side.)

SCALLOP QUENELLES WITH SHRIMP SAUCE

Quenelles are a type of poached dumpling that originally came from Nantua, France. Often you can find quenelles served with sauce Nantua, which is a cream seafood stock sauce. This is a variation of the classic French recipe.

SERVES 3, or 6 AS APPETIZERS

1   pound sea scallops
1   tablespoon minced fresh
     parsley
½   teaspoon salt
½   teaspoon pepper
2   cups water
½   cup white wine

1   recipe Shrimp Sauce (see
     Poached Halibut with
     Shrimp Sauce, page 58)
     Parsley sprigs, watercress,
     or capers (optional)

Rinse sea scallops in a colander, then put in a food processor. Process for 2 to 3 minutes, until they have a doughlike texture. Add parsley, salt, and pepper, and blend for another 10 to 20 seconds.

In a large sauté pan heat water and white wine until boiling. Mold scallop mixture into 3 separate football-shape figures (or 6 little ones for appetizers). Add to the boiling liquid and reduce heat to medium-high. Simmer for 2 to 3 minutes on each side. Remove from heat.

Place quenelles on middle of plate. Top with shrimp sauce. Garnish with parsley, watercress, or capers, then serve.

5

C R A B

STEAMED CRAB WITH DEVILED BUTTER

CRAB IMPERIAL

CRAB CAKES

SPINACH FETTUCINE WITH CRAB SAUCE

HUNGARIAN CRAB

CRAB CROQUETTES

CRAB FONDUE

CRAB AND ARTICHOKE HEART CASSEROLE

STEAMED CRAB WITH DEVILED BUTTER

Not only is the steamed crab by far the most simple recipe in this book, in my opinion it is one of the best. Especially good served with hot biscuits or fresh corn on the cob.

SERVES 2

DEVILED BUTTER

½   cup butter
1   teaspoon Dijon mustard
1   teaspoon wine vinegar
     Pinch cayenne pepper
1   teaspoon minced fresh
       parsley

2   1-pound crabs in shell
     (Dungeness preferred,
     but king crab works just
     as well)

In a saucepan melt butter over low heat with all of the above ingredients and set aside while steaming crab.

In a large deep pot steam crabs for 5 to 8 minutes, until thoroughly heated.

Immediately serve with deviled butter sauce on the side.

PREPARING CRAB

Have your local fish store clean your crabs. Some crabs have gills that are toxic, so unless you know how to clean them, I suggest letting the seafood dealer do it for you. However, here are instructions to clean, and "pick" them yourself.

To clean a crab, lift the little tab that runs under the crab's stomach. Continue to pull the tab until it starts to pull off the top shell of the crab. You will have to use your hands to pull the shell off, the tab alone will not do the job. Rinse and save the shell. The stomach cavity will have spongy-looking, off-white gills that lie on both sides. Remove the gills then all the body organs in the center of the crab and discard. Rinse the crab well under cold running water before cooking. Never throw the top shell away. It can be used as either a top to put back on the crab, stuffed, or used to make crab stock. You then will see white meat on both sides of the crab body divided by three pieces of cartilage into small sections. Pick the meat out of the body crevices and out of the legs by cracking the shell with seafood crackers or lightly using a hammer.

CRAB IMPERIAL

This recipe takes after its name, since it is so rich. Its creamy consistency goes well served on top of or alongside white rice.

SERVES 4

3 tablespoons butter
2 tablespoons flour
½ cup half-and-half
1 small shallot, minced
1 teaspoon Worcestershire
    sauce
2 slices white bread, crusts
    removed, cut into ½"
    cubes

½ cup mayonnaise
1 tablespoon lemon juice
½ teaspoon salt
    Few dashes freshly ground
    white pepper
1 pound crabmeat, cooked
    and picked (see sidebar)
    Dash paprika

Preheat oven to 450°F.

In a saucepan, melt 2 tablespoons butter over medium heat and mix with the flour. Slowly add half-and-half, stirring constantly so that it doesn't lump, until it thickens to a mud-thick consistency. Add shallot, Worcestershire sauce, and bread cubes. Set aside to cool.

When cool (about 15 minutes), gently fold in mayonnaise, lemon juice, salt, and white pepper.

Melt the remaining tablespoon butter in a skillet and toss with crabmeat. Mix with the sauce.

Put mixture either in a casserole dish or individual bowls, and bake for 10 minutes, or until slightly browned on top.

Garnish with a dash of paprika before serving.

CRAB CAKES

Crab cakes seem to be everyone's favorite, especially when served with a sweet chutney, or creamy Tarter Sauce. You could also serve slices of fruit such as papaya along the side, which not only goes well with the crab but looks nice on the plate with its bright orange color. Makes 6 to 8 cakes (or more for appetizers).

SERVES 2

1	pound crabmeat (snow, Dungeness, or blue crab preferred), cooked and picked (page 95)	A few dashes Tabasco sauce
1	egg, beaten	½ teaspoon dry mustard
¼	cup mayonnaise	½ cup fine dried bread crumbs
1	tablespoon minced fresh parsley	Generous sprinkle freshly ground white pepper
		Approximately 2 tablespoons butter

In a large mixing bowl combine crabmeat, egg, mayonnaise, parsley, Tabasco, and mustard. Mix well, then add bread crumbs. When mixed thoroughly, form into 6 to 8 round cakes.

In a sauté pan melt butter over medium-high heat, and sauté crab cakes for 3 to 4 minutes on each side, until golden brown. Serve.

SPINACH FETTUCINE WITH CRAB SAUCE

This is an active dish that requires timing. So be organized! Toss a salad ahead of time, have the garlic bread ready, and try to prepare in advance anything you plan to serve with dinner. The outcome is well worth it!

SERVES 6

1 12-ounce package spinach pasta	1 egg yolk
½ cup butter	⅔ cup light cream
1 cup crabmeat (Dungeness, blue, or snow crab preferred), cooked and picked (page 95)	½ cup grated Parmesan cheese
	2 tablespoons chopped fresh chives, or 1 teaspoon dried

Cook pasta according to the directions on the package. Be careful not to overcook.

Meanwhile, melt butter in a saucepan over low heat. Add crabmeat, stir, remove from heat, and set aside in the pan.

Mix egg yolk, cream, and cheese in a small bowl.

When pasta is done, drain well and transfer to a warm serving platter.

Add egg mixture to saucepan with butter and crab and heat over low flame, stirring sauce constantly until warm. Be very careful not to cook sauce too long, or else it will curdle. Pour over pasta and toss lightly. Garnish with chives and serve immediately.

HUNGARIAN CRAB

What a great dish to serve on a cold night! Serve warm over a bed of brown rice, perhaps with a nice bottle of hearty red wine.

SERVES 6

3   tablespoons olive oil
1   pound fresh mushrooms,
       quartered
3   cloves garlic, pressed
1   large onion, thinly sliced
       in rings
1   whole green pepper, cut
       into thin strips
3   scallions, chopped
2   tablespoons sherry
1   pound crabmeat, cooked
       and picked (page 95)
    Pinch cayenne papper
    Salt and black pepper to
       taste

2   tablespoons sweet
       Hungarian paprika
¾   cup sour cream

In a skillet heat olive oil and sauté mushrooms, garlic, onion, green pepper, and scallions until the onion is translucent. Add sherry and simmer for a few more minutes. Add crab, cayenne, salt and pepper, and paprika. Stir until the crab is thoroughly heated. Add the sour cream and serve when hot. Salt and pepper to taste.

CRAB CROQUETTES

If you have a deep fryer, making the croquettes will be easier than without. Makes approximately 14 to 16 croquettes.

SERVES 4

6	tablespoons butter	½	pound crabmeat, cooked
⅓	cup chopped onion		and picked (page 95)
¼	cup flour		Salt
	Dash Tabasco sauce	1	egg, beaten
½	teaspoon dry mustard		Fine dried bread crumbs
1	cup milk		Vegetable oil
1	teaspoon lemon juice		Lemon wedges
1	tablespoon minced fresh		
	parsley		

Preheat fryer to 375°F.

In a sauté pan melt butter over medium heat. Add onions and sauté until translucent, then blend in flour, Tabasco, mustard, and milk, stirring constantly until thick. Remove from heat, stir in lemon juice, parsley, and crabmeat. Season to taste and salt, then chill.

When chilled, shape into croquettes by hand then dip into beaten egg and roll in bread crumbs. (For helpful hints in making croquettes, see Seafood Croquettes, page 143.)

Cook croquettes in deep fryer for 3 to 5 minutes, until golden brown all over. If you don't have a deep fryer, heat 1½ cups vegetable oil in a sauté pan over medium-high heat, until hot enough to bubble when a tiny amount of water is sprinkled on it from your wet hand (make sure your hand is far away so oil does not spatter on you).

Set croquettes on a paper towel to drain. Serve hot with lemon wedges.

NOTE: The croquettes may be prepared in advance: Shape them and chill until ready to cook.

CRAB FONDUE

This is a fun meal when entertaining. Have the fondue pot in the middle of the table and let people eat at their own pace. You can serve this with a salad for a main course or serve alone as an appetizer.

1 8-ounce package cream cheese

6 ounces Gruyère cheese, grated (mozzarella may be substituted)

½ cup milk

¼ teaspoon cayenne pepper

¼ cup dry sherry or white wine (whichever you prefer)

1 pound crabmeat, cooked and picked (page 95) (snow, Dungeness, or blue preferred)

1 loaf of French bread, cut into 1½″ cubes

Combine cheeses, milk, cayenne, and sherry in fondue pot set on low heat. Stir until blended and smooth. Add crabmeat, stirring occasionally until hot but not boiling, 5 to 10 minutes.

Spear cubes of bread with fondue fork and dip in fondue pot. If mixture thickens while standing, stir in a little extra milk or sherry.

CRAB AND ARTICHOKE HEART CASSEROLE

A nice one-dish dinner that kids love!

SERVES 4–6

1	8-ounce package egg noodles	½	teaspoon salt
¼	cup butter	¼	teaspoon pepper
1	6-ounce jar marinated artichoke hearts	¼	cup sherry
1½	cups sour cream	1	pound crabmeat, cooked and picked (page 95)
1	cup heavy cream	¼	cup grated Parmesan cheese

Preheat oven to 350°F.

Cook noodles in a pot of boiling water according to directions on package. Drain.

Return pasta to large pot and melt butter over it, tossing well.

Slice artichoke hearts into small pieces and add with canned liquid to noodles; toss. Mix in remaining ingredients. Pour into casserole dish and bake for 20 minutes. Serve.

CLAMS AND OYSTERS

LINGUINI WITH WHITE CLAM SAUCE

CLAM FRITTERS

CAPELLINI WITH RED CLAM SAUCE

LINGUINI WITH WHITE CLAM, SUN-DRIED TOMATO, AND
WILD MUSHROOM SAUCE

BROILED OYSTERS TOPPED WITH SUN-DRIED TOMATO SAUCE

FRIED OYSTERS

BAKED ZUCCHINI STUFFED WITH OYSTERS AND WILD
MUSHROOMS

LINGUINI WITH WHITE CLAM SAUCE

Oysters and clams may be enjoyed all year round and are readily available at seafood markets. This clam sauce freezes beautifully.

SERVES 4

CLAM SAUCE

2	tablespoons olive oil	4	tablespoons minced fresh parsley
⅓	cup chopped scallions		
2	tablespoons pressed garlic	1	1-pound package linguini or spaghetti
1	cup clam juice		
¼	cup white wine		Grated Parmesan cheese (optional)
¼	teaspoon white pepper		
2	tablespoons butter		
1	cup minced, cooked cherrystone clams (see sidebar)		

Heat olive oil in a saucepan and cook scallions and garlic over low heat until tender. Stir in clam juice, wine, white pepper, and butter. Raise heat to medium-high. Bring to a boil then reduce heat. Simmer uncovered for about 5 minutes, or until liquid has reduced to almost half. Add clams and parsley and cook until clams are heated through.

Meanwhile, in a pot of boiling water cook pasta according to directions on package. Drain.

Toss clam sauce with pasta and top with Parmesan cheese, if you like. Serve immediately, since this dish gets cold fast.

PREPARING CLAMS

When a recipe calls for minced cooked clams, I would buy cherrystones. Cherrystones do not require the removal of the long black neck casing that steamers have, and this saves time and effort.

However, if you're not using cherrystones, you'll need to shuck the clams: Before shucking clams, if you have the time, you can soak them in salted water for an hour or two so that they will purge any sand they may contain (a tablespoon to every quart).

Shucking clams (and oysters) is not an easy job, but don't be intimidated, be patient and careful when working. Put a rubber glove on your left hand to hold the mollusk (if you are right-handed; do just the opposite if left-handed). Let the point of the mollusk face you and place your left hand on top of that. Then place the rounder side of the shell on the table to better hold the precious flavorful juices. Insert an opener, which, if not specially purchased, might be a can opener or screwdriver, between the shells of the mollusk. In a small twisting-of-the-wrist motion lightly wiggle the blade between the shells toward the top shell, so that you can slice the strong muscle holding the shells together. Remember that shellfish are easier to shuck when they are well chilled, even if it means popping them in the freezer for fifteen minutes before preparation.

Steam clams in a large pot of boiling water for twelve to fourteen minutes, until their shells are fully open. Drain in a colander and let cool. Then remove clams from their shells and mince the meat on a cutting board.

CLAM FRITTERS

Fritters are a favorite Southern recipe. They can be served as an appetizer, main dish, or easy lunch. This goes well served with Cocktail and Tartar Sauce (see Chapter 10, "Sauces and Dips").

SERVES 2—ABOUT 10 FRITTERS

1 cup flour	1 egg, beaten
½ teaspoon baking powder	⅓ cup clam juice
Dash pepper	1 tablespoon minced fresh
1 dozen cherrystone clams,	parsley
shucked (page 109) and	Dash Tabasco sauce
then chopped coarsely to	
size of peas	

Heat deep fryer to 375°F.

In a large bowl blend flour, baking powder, and pepper. Add remaining ingredients and mix well.

Drop the batter carefully, a spoonful at a time, into deep fryer. Fry until golden brown, about 2 to 3 minutes. Drain fritters on paper towels and serve.

CAPELLINI WITH RED CLAM SAUCE

This hearty red sauce served over delicate pasta makes an interesting and delicious combination.

SERVES 2

RED CLAM SAUCE

1 10-ounce can plum
     tomatoes
2 tablespoons olive oil
1 clove garlic, pressed
½ cup onion, chopped
¼ cup green pepper, chopped
1 bay leaf
¼ cup chopped fresh basil
1 cup chopped, cooked
     cherrystone clams (see
     page 109)

¼ teaspoon salt
¼ teaspoon freshly ground
     pepper
⅓ cup red wine

1 8-ounce package capellini
     (angle hair pasta)
   Grated Parmesan cheese
     (optional)

Slice tomatoes in half and remove the seeds. In a blender or food processor blend tomatoes at high speed for approximately 1 minute.

In a large skillet heat olive oil over medium heat. Add garlic and onion; sauté for approximately 3 minutes. Pour pureed tomatoes in skillet, along with green pepper, bay leaf, basil, clams, salt, pepper, and wine. Simmer for 30 minutes over medium-low heat.

While sauce is simmering, cook pasta in a pot of boiling water according to package directions, being careful not to overcook. Drain.

Top pasta with clam sauce and serve. Sprinkle with Parmesan cheese, if you like.

LINGUINI WITH WHITE CLAM, SUN-DRIED TOMATO, AND WILD MUSHROOM SAUCE

My favorite pasta recipe—the combination of bright red sun-dried tomatoes and dark mushrooms spread over the pasta is truly beautiful.

SERVES 4

¼	pound sun-dried tomatoes	1	cup clam juice
2	tablespoons olive oil	⅓	cup white wine
2	tablespoons butter	¼	teaspoon freshly ground pepper
2	tablespoons pressed garlic		
¼	cup chopped scallions	1	tablespoon minced fresh parsley, plus extra for garnish
¼	pound black forest mushrooms (regular mushrooms may be substituted)		
		1	1-pound package linguini
1	cup minced, cooked clams (page 109)		

Place dried tomatoes in boiling water, turn off heat, and let soak for at least 30 minutes. Rinse and drain in strainer before using.

In a saucepan heat olive oil and butter and sauté garlic, scallions, mushrooms, and tomatoes over low heat for approximately 5 minutes. Then add clams, clam juice, white wine, pepper, and parsley. Raise heat to medium-high and bring to a boil, then reduce heat and let simmer gently, covered, for 15 minutes.

Meanwhile, in a pot of boiling water cook pasta according to package directions. Drain.

Place pasta on a warm serving platter and top with clam sauce. Garnish with minced parsley and serve.

BROILED OYSTERS TOPPED WITH SUN-DRIED TOMATO SAUCE

I like to serve this rich oyster dish with mild accompaniments, such as rice pilaf tossed with chopped scallions and asparagus spears.

SERVES 4

Rock salt
2 dozen oysters, shucked
   (you can ask your
   seafood store to do this
   for you or see page 109)

GARNISH

   Parsley sprigs
   Lemon slices

SAUCE

2 tablespoons butter
4 ounces sun-dried tomatoes
   in oil, drained and
   chopped
¼ cup chopped roasted red
   bell peppers (see Note)
1 tablespoon balsamic
   vinegar

Preheat oven to 550°F (Broil).

Fill 2 small broiler pans with ½″ layer of rock salt. Place the shucked oysters on the salt and broil about 2″ from heat for 1 to 3 minutes, until oysters are sizzling on top but not brown. Remove oysters from oven and set aside while you make tomato sauce.

In sauté pan melt butter over medium heat and add tomatoes, peppers, vinegar. Stir for approximately 2 minutes, until sauce is heated through. Carefully spoon over oysters.

Place 6 oysters on each plate. Serve with the accompaniments you like. Garnish with parsley sprigs and thin lemon slices on the side.

NOTE: To prepare ¼ cup chopped roasted peppers you will need 1 medium red bell or red Italian pepper. Roast the pepper either on the outdoor grill over medium-hot coals, on top of a gas stove, or on a cookie sheet in the oven until the outer skin is charred and black. Put the pepper into a small brown paper bag and let set until cool, 20 to 30 minutes. Remove the pepper from the bag, peel off the black skin, slice the pepper in half, remove the seeds, and discard the skins and the seeds. You now have a delicious roasted pepper ready to use any way you like.

FRIED OYSTERS

Crispy batter on the outside, tender oyster inside, a favorite of many when cooked to perfection. Serve with Cocktail Sauce and Tartar Sauce (see Chapter 10, "Sauces and Dips").

SERVES 3

2   cups flour
2   teaspoons salt
1   teaspoon freshly ground
      pepper
3   eggs
1   cup heavy cream

1   cup milk
3   dozen oysters, shucked (ask
      your seafood store to do
      it for you or see page
      109)
About 2 cups vegetable oil

In a shallow dish mix flour, salt, and pepper together.

In another shallow dish whisk eggs, cream, and milk together.

Take each oyster and dip in egg mixture then dredge in flour, 2 or 3 times, until well coated.

In a deep skillet heat ½″ oil over medium-high heat to 350°F. Fry oysters for 1 to 2 minutes each side, until golden brown.

Transfer with tongs to paper towels to drain.

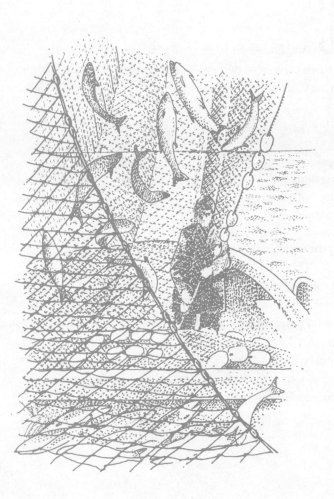

BAKED ZUCCHINI STUFFED WITH OYSTERS AND WILD MUSHROOMS

This is a great recipe for zucchini, a vegetable available year-round.

SERVES 6

3	medium-size zucchini	2	cups shucked oysters
3	tablespoons butter		(page 109), liquid
3	cloves garlic, pressed		drained
1	cup fresh chopped	1½	cups fresh bread crumbs
	shiitake mushrooms	¼	teaspoon dried oregano

Preheat oven to 375°F. Lightly butter a baking dish.

Scrub and trim zucchini; then halve lengthwise. Scoop out the pulp and discard. Set zucchini halves aside.

In a large skillet melt butter over low heat, add garlic, mushrooms, and oysters. Sauté for 3 to 5 minutes. Add bread crumbs and oregano, then toss over low heat for 1 to 2 minutes, until well blended. Remove from heat.

Arrange zucchini in baking dish. Stuff with oyster stuffing and bake for 20 to 25 minutes, until zucchini are tender when pierced with a fork.

Serve hot and enjoy.

7

S H R I M P

SHRIMP FLORENTINE WITH DILL SAUCE

SHRIMP TERIYAKI

SPANISH-STYLE SHRIMP

CURRIED SHRIMP

SHRIMP JAMBALAYA

SHRIMP OR CRAB NEWBURG

SWEET AND SOUR SHRIMP

GUACAMOLE-SHRIMP TORTILLAS

SHRIMP SCAMPI

STIR-FRY SHRIMP

SHRIMP CAPELLINI

SHRIMP FLORENTINE WITH DILL SAUCE

An Italian favorite that originated in Florence with a sauce that originated from my own kitchen—a great combination!

SERVES 6

DILL SAUCE

4	tablespoons butter	2	tablespoons minced fresh chives
1	teaspoon crushed or minced garlic	1½	cups Fish Stock (page 178) or chicken stock
3	tablespoons minced shallots	1	pound medium-size shrimp in their shells
1½	cups heavy cream	¼	cup dry vermouth
1	teaspoon flour	1	pound fresh spinach, washed and stemmed
3	tablespoons minced fresh dill		

GARNISH

Dill sprigs
Lemon wedges

In a sauté pan melt 2 tablespoons butter over low heat and add the garlic and shallots. Sauté until soft, approximately 4 minutes. In a bowl blend cream, flour, dill, and chives. Mix in garlic and shallots.

In a large pot bring stock to a boil, add shrimp and cook in the stock uncovered over medium heat until done, 3 to 5 minutes. Be careful not to overcook shrimp or they will lose their texture. The shrimp will be done when they lose their translucent color inside and become white throughout. Remove shrimp, either by straining in a colander over a bowl, or with a slotted spoon, but save the broth.

Add vermouth to broth and bring back to a boil over medium heat, reducing it by half, about 10 minutes.

Meanwhile, peel and devein shrimp (see sidebar). It is preferable to leave tails on, as the color contrast between the spinach and the bright tails enhances the dish.

Once the stock is reduced to half, add cream mixture. Let sauce reduce down half again, frequently stirring, then cover and keep warm.

Cook spinach with 2 tablespoons butter by steaming in a vegetable steamer or in an inch of boiling water until wilted, 2 to 3 minutes. Drain. Make a bed or a well with the spinach on a platter. Spoon sauce in center and top it with shrimp. Garnish with sprigs of dill and lemon wedges.

PREPARING SHRIMP

When a recipe calls for cooked, peeled, deveined shrimp, buy the amount of shrimp (1 pound = 21 to 25 medium shrimp) called for in the recipe raw and in the shell at your local seafood store. Peel the shrimp by grabbing the legs in one hand and lightly holding the end of the tail with the other. Pull the legs up and around the body of the shrimp so that the shell follows. Then make a shallow cut lengthwise down the back of the shrimp and rinse out the sandy vein under cold running water.

To cook 1 pound, in a deep pot bring 2 cups water to a boil over high heat. Add shrimp, cover, and reduce heat to medium; simmer for 5 to 8 minutes.

SHRIMP TERIYAKI

When in doubt, make Shrimp Teriyaki. Everyone loves it. It goes well with a nice seasonal tossed salad and either corn on the cob or baked potatoes.

SERVES 2

½   cup rice vinegar
¼   cup soy sauce
½   cup brown sugar
¼   cup sesame oil
 1   pound medium-size
       shrimp, peeled and
       deveined (see page 123)

In a mixing bowl combine vinegar, soy sauce, sugar, and oil. Mix well.

Add shrimp to marinade and let stand at room temperature for 30 minutes.

Light a barbecue grill, or preheat oven to 550°F (Broil).

Grill shrimp for 8 to 10 minutes. You can also broil the shrimp. If you do, you should baste frequently with the marinade and broil on broiler pan for approximately 2 minutes each side.

SPANISH-STYLE SHRIMP

A little spicy, but if you prefer it hotter, add Tabasco sauce to taste. Serve over steamed white rice.

3 tablespoons olive oil
1 shallot, minced
1 green pepper, cut into
     ½" squares
1 cup canned plum
     tomatoes
1 8-ounce can tomato sauce
½ teaspoon garlic powder
½ teaspoon celery salt
1 tablespoon minced fresh
     parsley
1–2 teaspoons Tabasco sauce
     (optional)

2 pounds medium-size
     shrimp, peeled and
     deveined (page 123)

In a skillet heat olive oil and sauté shallot and green pepper over medium heat until shallot is translucent. Add the remaining ingredients, except shrimp, and simmer over low heat, covered, for 1 hour.

Add shrimp to sauce and simmer for another 15 minutes, uncovered, until shrimp are cooked.

CURRIED SHRIMP

Curry originated in Madras, India. It is not an actual spice, but a blend of many spices including cumin, turmeric, cardamom, mace, ginger, and red and black peppers. Some curries may contain as many as 15 different spices! Curry ranges from mild to very hot and can actually lower body temperature when it is very hot.

Serve your curry as the Indians do—with dishes of condiments, such as grated coconut, sliced bananas, sliced tomatoes, diced raw onion, plain yogurt, pineapple, and, of course, chutney, sometimes made with mangoes or papaya. Serve shrimp over hot steamed rice.

SERVES 4

2   tablespoons butter
2   pounds medium-size
       shrimp in their shells

CURRY SAUCE

2   tablespoons minced onion
3   tablespoons honey
2   teaspoons curry powder
¼   cup Dijon mustard
2   teaspoons lemon juice
1   teaspoon minced fresh
       parsley

In a skillet melt butter over medium-low heat. Sauté shrimp and onion for 4 to 5 minutes, stirring frequently so butter doesn't burn.

In a small mixing bowl combine sauce ingredients, then set aside. Preheat broiler.

Peel and devein shrimp (see page 123), then rinse and layer in a casserole dish. Top with the curry sauce. Broil for 5 to 8 minutes, basting a few times.

SHRIMP JAMBALAYA

This is surely the perfect dish for a large informal gathering. Originally Creole in origin, Jambalaya is a favorite summertime casserole served with a colorful fruit salad.

SERVES 4

4 slices bacon	1 cup chopped fresh
⅓ cup chopped onion	tomatoes
½ red bell pepper, coarsely	1¼ cups water
chopped into ¼" pieces	⅓ cup tomato juice
½ green pepper, coarsely	1 clove garlic, pressed
chopped into ¼" pieces	Pinch cayenne pepper
2 tablespoons flour	1 teaspoon chili powder
1 cup cooked shrimp,	1 cup uncooked white rice
peeled and deveined	
(page 123)	

In a large skillet fry bacon over medium-high heat until extra crispy. Take out and crumble when cool.

Pour bacon grease into a large pan and sauté onion and red and green peppers until onion is translucent and slightly browned. Add flour and mix until there are no lumps left. Add crumbled bacon, and shrimp. Stir until well blended. Add tomatoes, water, tomato juice, garlic, cayenne, and chili powder; stir until well blended and at the point of boiling.

Add rice, cover, and reduce heat to a simmer. Let cook for 20 to 25 minutes, until rice has absorbed most of liquid. Fluff with a fork and serve.

SHRIMP OR CRAB NEWBURG

In this elegant classic dish, the use of sherry is optional. Newburg is traditionally served over white rice or toast.

SERVES 4

¼	cup butter	½	teaspoon paprika
3	eggs	½	teaspoon grated nutmeg
1	cup heavy cream	½	teaspoon white pepper
¼	cup sherry (optional)	2	cups cleaned cooked
1	tablespoon orange zest		shrimp or crabmeat (see
	(optional)		page 123 or 95)

In a double boiler melt butter.

In a small bowl mix eggs and cream together well. Add sherry and orange zest, if desired, paprika, nutmeg, and white pepper, stirring until well blended. Slowly add this mixture in a stream to melted butter while stirring or whisking constantly.

When well blended, add shrimp or crabmeat. Continue to stir until thickened to a creamy mud-thick sauce. Serve.

SWEET AND SOUR SHRIMP

A tantalizing twist to sweet and sour pork. Serve over or with white rice.

SERVES 4

1	pound medium-size shrimp, peeled and deveined (page 123)
8	scallions, cut diagonally into ¼" pieces
1	cup dry white wine
2	tablespoons sesame oil

SWEET AND SOUR SAUCE

½	cup pineapple juice
2	tablespoons sesame or vegetable oil
¼	cup brown sugar
⅓	cup ketchup
1	teaspoon soy sauce
¼	cup cider vinegar
¾	cup water mixed with 1 teaspoon cornstarch

Place shrimp and scallions in white wine to marinate while you prepare sauce.

In a saucepan mix sauce ingredients and place over low heat.

Bring to a boil, reduce heat, and stir until slightly thickened. Set aside.

Remove shrimp and scallions from wine.

In a skillet heat sesame oil over high flame. When hot, quickly stir-fry shrimp and scallions until just cooked but not overdone, 2 to 3 minutes.

Add sauce, cover, and let simmer for 5 to 10 minutes. Serve.

GUACAMOLE-SHRIMP TORTILLAS

Perfect for casual entertaining and round-robin days on the tennis court. Teen-agers love it. Serve with Sangria for the older crowd. Nice accompaniments are bowls filled with sour cream, chopped tomatoes, minced onions, and salsa to pass around the table. Makes 4 tortillas.

SERVES 2

2   very ripe avocados (see Note), peeled and seeded
¼   cup finely minced onion
¼   cup chopped tomatoes, peeled and seeded (page 64)
½   teaspoon chili powder
1   tablespoon wine vinegar
    Pinch cayenne pepper

½   teaspoon garlic powder
½   cup chopped cooked shrimp, peeled and deveined (page 123)
4   flour tortillas
½   cup grated Monterey Jack or Swiss cheese
    Cherry tomatoes or thin strips of red bell pepper

In a mixing bowl mash avocados with a fork until a lumpy paste is formed. Add onions, tomatoes, chili powder, vinegar, cayenne, and garlic. Mix gently but well.

Add shrimp and coat with guacamole. Spread on tortillas and roll them up.

Heat broiler and lightly grease a casserole. Place tortillas in casserole with seam side down. Top with grated cheese. Broil until the cheese is melted and slightly browned, about 2 minutes. The guacamole should not be hot, only the cheese.

Serve immediately. Garnish with cherry tomatoes or thin strips of red bell pepper.

NOTE: To ripen avocados, place in a brown paper bag in a warm, dry place for a couple of days.

SHRIMP SCAMPI

For garlic lovers only. This traditional Italian dish works well as both a gourmet dinner or an easy Sunday supper.

SERVES 4

¼	cup lightly salted butter	1 pound medium-size
3	teaspoons pressed garlic	shrimp, peeled and
¼	cup chopped scallions	deveined (page 128)
1	large tomato, diced	2–3 tablespoons grated
¼	cup white wine	Parmesan cheese

In sauté pan melt butter over low heat. Add garlic, scallions, and tomato. Increase heat to medium-high and sauté for 2 to 3 minutes, then add wine. When hot, add shrimp and sauté until cooked, approximately 5 minutes.

Sprinkle Parmesan cheese over shrimp and serve.

STIR-FRY SHRIMP

The newest in wok cookery—fast, easy, low-cal, fun, and healthy. Serve on top of steaming white rice.

SERVES 4

1 pound medium-size shrimp, peeled and deveined (page 123)	¼ cup sliced red bell pepper, cut into approximately ½" square pieces
¼ cup soy sauce	¼ cup sliced carrots, cut into approximately ½" square pieces
2 tablespoons dry sherry or white wine	1½ cups chopped broccoli, cut into approximately ½" square pieces
Dash Tabasco sauce or to taste	
1 teaspoon cornstarch	
1 teaspoon sugar	1 cup sliced mushrooms, cut into approximately ½" square pieces
1 tablespoon Dijon mustard	
1 teaspoon chopped garlic	1 cup chopped scallions, cut into approximately ½" square pieces
1 tablespoon miso paste (found in specialty or Oriental stores)	
¼ cup sesame oil	¼ cup toasted sesame seeds Thin lemon slices (optional)

In a large mixing bowl combine shrimp, soy sauce, sherry, Tabasco, cornstarch, sugar, mustard, garlic, and miso paste. Let stand for 15 minutes.

In a wok heat sesame oil and add marinated fish mixture, vegetables, and sesame seeds. Cook over high heat, stirring gently, until vegetables are tender but not overcooked, approximately 5 minutes.

SHRIMP CAPELLINI

One of my own personal favorite dishes. I like to serve this with a large tossed salad.

SERVES 4

1	8-ounce package capellini (angel hair pasta)	1	8-ounce can whole tomatoes in their own juice
½	cup butter		
2	cloves garlic, pressed	1	pound medium-size shrimp, peeled, deveined, and cooked (page 123)
2	tablespoons minced fresh parsley		
1½	cups clam juice		
1½	cups white wine	¼	cup grated Parmesan cheese

Cook pasta in a pot of boiling water according to the directions on the package. Drain and set aside.

In a sauté pan melt butter over low heat with garlic and parsley, then add clam juice and white wine and let cook over low heat.

Meanwhile, drain tomatoes. Chop tomatoes on cutting board and strain one more time under low running cold water to remove seeds. Add tomatoes to sauce. Add shrimp and pasta. Toss well.

Transfer onto platter, sprinkle with Parmesan cheese, and serve.

S E A F O O D
COMBINATIONS

SEAFOOD SOUFFLÉ

SPICY ALASKAN CIOPPINO

SEAFOOD CROQUETTES

ALASKAN SEVICHE

SEAFOOD FONDUE

ALASKAN SEAFOOD CRUMB PIE

SEAFOOD FETTUCINE

SEAFOOD SOUFFLÉ

Easier than it sounds. Perfect as an elegant luncheon or dinner with salad to accompany it. Your friends will think you have worked for hours!

SERVES 6

3 tablespoons butter
3 tablespoons flour
1 cup milk
Dash freshly ground white pepper
Dash grated nutmeg
1 tablespoon minced fresh parsley
3 eggs, separated, beaten separately

¼ cup cooked shrimp, peeled, deveined, and chopped (page 123)
1 cup crabmeat, cooked and picked (page 95)
½ cup cooked bay scallops (page 82)
Salt and black pepper to taste

Preheat oven to 350°F. Grease well a 1½-quart casserole or soufflé dish.

In a skillet melt butter over low heat and blend with flour. Gradually add milk and stir over low heat until mud-thick and smooth. Add white pepper, nutmeg, and parsley.

In a small mixing bowl add beaten egg yolks and stir a little sauce in to prevent yolks from cooking too fast. Then slowly, stirring constantly, add yolk mixture to remaining sauce on the stove with heat off.

Add seafood and fold in beaten egg whites. Add salt and pepper. Pour into casserole or soufflé dish. Bake for 45 minutes, so that soufflé is firm in center.

Serve immediately after cooking—soufflés start to deflate when removed from oven.

SPICY ALASKAN CIOPPINO

The closest thing Alaskans have to minestrone. It's all fresh seafood instead of vegetables and most definitely a meal in itself. Serve with garlic bread on the side.

SERVES 8

½ cup olive oil	1 ½-pound halibut fillet, cut into 1″ cubes
2 teaspoons pressed garlic	
1½ cups minced onions	½ pound steamer clams in their shells, well rinsed in colander
¾ cup chopped green pepper	
¼ cup minced fresh parsley	½ pound shrimp, peeled and deveined (page 123)
⅛ teaspoon cayenne pepper or to taste	
1½ cups coarsely chopped canned tomatoes, drained	½ pound bay scallops, quickly rinsed and drained
2 teaspoons tomato paste	1½ pounds king crabmeat (bought cooked, and served in the shell) (page 95)
3 cups clam juice	
1 cup red wine	
1 teaspoon dried oregano	
1 teaspoon dried basil	¼ cup chopped scallions
1 teaspoon sugar	
Salt and pepper to taste	

In a heavy skillet heat oil over low heat. Add garlic, onion, and green pepper. Stir until softened, approximately 5 minutes.

Transfer to a large soup kettle and add parsley, cayenne, tomatoes, tomato paste, clam juice, red wine, oregano, basil, sugar, salt and pepper. Bring to a boil over medium-high heat. Make sure everything is well blended with no lumps of tomato paste.

When boiling, add halibut, scallops, clams, and shrimp. Cover and cook for 5 to 8 minutes. Add crabmeat (or crab), reduce heat to low, and simmer for 10 to 15 minutes, covered, until ready to serve.

Sprinkle with scallions for garnish.

SEAFOOD CROQUETTES

For this recipe salmon, shrimp, scallops, clams, king crab, or Dungeness crab may be used.

Croquettes have a crunchy outside and are soft on the inside. The mixture for the inside of the croquette must be chilled and then hand-made into a ball or cone shape. If you have problems with the mixture holding its shape, you will have to add some flour or more potatoes. It helps to make sure that the seafood you add is drained of all excess liquid and patted dry. It is also helpful to let the breading on the outside of the croquette dry about an hour before deep-frying. Makes approximately 24 croquettes. You can serve them just as they are or top with a white sauce or tomato sauce.

SERVES 6

CROQUETTES

1   cup poached salmon (page 32)
1   cup cooked shrimp, peeled and deveined (page 123)
1   cup cooked bay scallops (page 82)
3   cups mashed potatoes
2   eggs, beaten
½   teaspoon garlic salt
½   teaspoon white pepper
1   teaspoon minced fresh parsley

BREADING

2   eggs, slightly beaten
2   cups fine bread crumbs or crushed crispy cereal

In a large bowl mix croquette ingredients, cover, and chill thoroughly in the refrigerator for approximately 2 hours.

When seafood mixture is thoroughly chilled, shape into little cones or balls.

Bread each croquette by dipping in eggs and then rolling in crumbs. For best results, set them out to dry for 1 hour.

Preheat deep fryer to 375°F.

Fry the croquettes for 3 to 5 minutes, just until golden brown. Set them out to drain on paper towels before serving. If you do not have a deep fryer, heat oil in a large skillet over medium-high heat. Fill skillet a quarter full with oil. Fry croquettes 1 or 2 at a time transferring back and forth with a slotted spoon and turning them often so they are evenly browned.

ALASKAN SEVICHE

Seviche is a unique summertime dish. The seafood is actually cooked by the vinegar and lemon juice, so it needs a day to "marinate." Perfect for warm evenings, it also can be made a day or two in advance and stored in the refrigerator until ready to serve.

SERVES 4

1   ½-pound fresh king
     salmon fillet, cut into
     bite-size cubes
1   ½-pound fresh halibut
     fillet, cubed
½   pound fresh shrimp,
     peeled and deveined
     (page 123)
½   pound fresh sea scallops
1½ cups white wine vinegar

1½ cups water
1   large tarragon stem
1   bay leaf
1   medium onion, thinly
     sliced
1   tablespoon black
     peppercorns
     Juice from ½ lemon
1   tablespoon sugar

Place seafood in a large ceramic bowl. Add remaining ingredients and toss well. Cover and place in the refrigerator for at least 24 hours.

Before serving, discard bay leaf and tarragon stem.

SERVING SUGGESTIONS: Seviche may be served in a bowl along with its juices. Another way to serve is to remove the seafood with a slotted spoon and serve on a bed of white rice that has been tossed with scallions, or on a bed of lettuce greens.

SEAFOOD FONDUE

This is a fine dinner with many different kinds of seafood—great to serve for a dinner party. There are two types of batter to choose from. I often use both the Egg Batter and Beer Batter on the table.

SERVES 8

½ pound medium-size
    shrimp, peeled and
    deveined (page 123)
½ pound bay scallops

1 ½-pound halibut fillet, cut
    into bite-size pieces
1 ½-pound salmon fillet, cut
    into bite-size pieces

EGG BATTER

6 eggs
½ cup milk
1 cup flour
1 teaspoon salt

1 recipe Beer Batter (see
    Beer-Battered Halibut,
    page 60)

Heat oil in fondue pot to 375°F.

Arrange seafood on a large tray on a bed of lettuce.

To make egg batter you will need 2 bowls. In first bowl mix eggs and milk. In second bowl mix flour and salt.

Dip chunks of seafood in egg bowl then in flour. Cook in fondue pot for 30 to 60 seconds, until golden brown.

Or dip seafood chunks in beer batter then cook in fondue pot for 30 to 60 seconds, until golden.

Let fish cool before eating.

People will pass the seafood around the table and eat what they feel like at their own pace. I like to serve the fondue with little bowls of different sauces, such as Tartar, Cocktail, and Mustard Sauce (see Chapter 10, "Sauces and Dips").

ALASKAN SEAFOOD CRUMB PIE

A delicious recipe that blends shrimp, scallops, and salmon.

SERVES 6

CRUST	FILLING

CRUST

¼ cup butter
2   tablespoons minced onions
2   cloves garlic, pressed
2   cups soft bread crumbs
½   teaspoon celery salt
    Dash salt and pepper

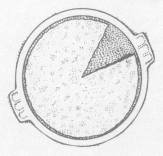

FILLING

⅓   cup butter
6   tablespoons flour
1   cup half-and-half
1   cup Fish Stock (page 178)
    or chicken stock
1   egg, well beaten
    Dash celery salt
½   cup cooked shrimp, peeled
    and deveined (page 123)
½   cup cooked scallops (page
    82)
½   cup poached salmon meat
    (page 32)
¼   cup dry bread crumbs
    mixed with 2
    tablespoons melted
    butter

Preheat oven to 375°F.

In a sauté pan melt butter and sauté onion and garlic over medium heat until onion is soft.

In a bowl mix garlic and onion with remaining crust ingredients and press into a 10″ pie pan. Bake for 10 minutes, until slightly brown and toasted. Remove crust from oven and raise heat to 400°.

In a heavy skillet melt butter and blend flour in well.

In a mixing bowl blend half-and-half, stock, egg, and celery salt. Add to butter and flour slowly, stirring constantly. Gently add seafood and simmer for a few more minutes, until mixture is slightly thickened.

Pour mixture into baked crust. Top with buttered bread crumbs. Bake for 25 to 30 minutes. Remove from oven and let stand for 10 minutes before serving.

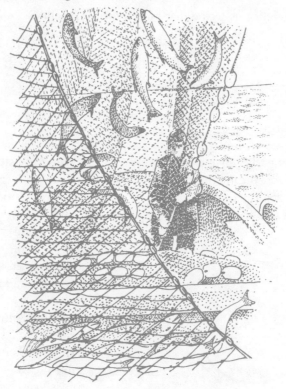

SEAFOOD FETTUCINE

Everyone loves this fettucine. Be creative and use any kind of pasta you like.

SERVES 4

1	cup small shrimp, peeled and deveined (page 123)	½	cup butter
1	cup bay scallops	1	egg yolk
1	tablespoon olive oil	⅔	cup light cream
1	clove garlic, minced	½	cup grated Parmesan cheese
4	cups water	1	teaspoon minced fresh parsley
1	1-pound package fettucine		

Wash shrimp and scallops, drain well, and pat dry.

In a saucepan heat olive oil and garlic over medium heat. Add shrimp and scallops. Sauté for 3 to 4 minutes, being careful not to overcook. Scallops should still be opaque in the center. Set aside.

Boil water in large deep pot and, when boiling, add pasta and cook for approximately 6 minutes. You will want to make sure of your timing at this point, so that pasta and sauce are done at the same time.

In a saucepan melt butter over low heat. Add shrimp and scallops and keep warm.

In a bowl mix egg yolk and cream until well blended.

Drain pasta and place on a large, warm serving platter. Mix egg and cream in sauté pan over medium heat. Then add butter, seafood, and cheese.

When well blended, pour over pasta and toss. Serve immediately.

9

APPETIZERS AND HORS D'OEUVRES

CRAB MELT ON TOAST POINTS

SCALLOPS WRAPPED IN BACON

FRIED CLAMS

CLAMS CASINO

SALMON PÂTÉ

SEAFOOD TERRINE

CRAB LOUIS

BROILED CHERRYSTONE CLAMS

CRAB MELT ON TOAST POINTS

Great finger food to pass around at parties. These are easy to serve and not very messy.

SERVES 6

2   tablespoons butter
2   cloves garlic, pressed
1   teaspoon minced fresh
    parsley
2   tablespoons flour
1   cup light cream

1   egg yolk
½   pound crabmeat, cooked
    and picked (page 95)
6   slices thin white bread,
    crusts removed
    Grated Parmesan cheese

Preheat oven to 550°F (Broil).

In a small saucepan melt butter with garlic and parsley over low heat. Remove from heat and whisk in flour. Add cream and beat until creamy. Return to low heat, slowly add egg yolk to mixture while whisking briskly. Stir constantly until a thick, puddinglike consistency, approximately 1 minute. Remove from heat. Add crabmeat and blend thoroughly. Set aside.

To cut toast points from bread slices, make two diagonal slices that cross, leaving 4 triangular pieces from 1 bread slice. Top each piece with crab mixture. Sprinkle lightly with Parmesan cheese.

Place under broiler for approximately 30 seconds, until golden on top. Serve hot.

SCALLOPS WRAPPED IN BACON

A version of "Angels on Horseback" (hot dogs wrapped in bacon). You may serve the scallops plain, or try Mustard Sauce (see Chapter 10, "Sauces and Dips") or a sesame dressing.

SERVES 2–3

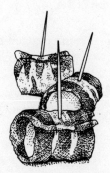

1   pound (10–20) large sea
      scallops
    10–20 bacon slices
    2–4 tablespoons brown
      sugar

Preheat oven to 550°F (Broil).

In a skillet partially cook bacon slices so that they are still soft and pliable, but not crisp. Pour out any excess grease in pan and discard. Sprinkle bacon with brown sugar, set aside.

Cut any large scallops into bite-size pieces. Wrap a strip of bacon around each scallop. Use a toothpick to hold in place.

Broil until bacon is crisp, approximately 2 minutes, and serve.

FRIED CLAMS

A perennial boardwalk favorite. Serve with tartar sauce, cocktail sauce, and lemon wedges.

SERVES 4

1   pound cleaned razor clams
(See page 109);
cherrystone clams—
which you don't have to
clean—may be
substituted. Ask your
seafood store to shuck the
clams for your
convenience.

2   beaten eggs
1   cup all-purpose flour
2   cups vegetable oil
Garlic powder

Rinse the clams and pat dry. If razor clams are used, take a meat pounder and gently pound the necks of the clams.

Dip the clams in eggs and then dredge in flour until clams are completely coated with flour. Lay them on a piece of waxed paper. Continue the process until all are done.

In a large, heavy pan heat vegetable oil and a dash of garlic powder over medium-high heat.

Fry clams until golden brown, 4 to 5 minutes, turning frequently. (Cook clams in a few batches, it's easier than trying to fry them all at once.) Place clams on paper towels when removing from oil, to let drain, and serve while still hot.

CLAMS CASINO

Regardless of the name—the gamble is well worth the risk!

SERVES 6

3 dozen cherrystone clams
¼ cup minced shallots
¼ cup minced pimientoes
6 slices bacon

GARNISH

Parsley sprigs
Lemon wedges

Preheat oven to 550°F (Broil).

Rinse clams under cold running water in colander then open on the half shell and place on broiler pan.

In a mixing bowl combine minced shallots and pimientoes. Sprinkle approximately ½ teaspoon of mixture on each clam.

Cut pieces of bacon just large enough to cover the top of each clam. Put bacon on clams and place under broiler until bacon is cooked, 5 to 8 minutes.

Garnish with parsley and lemon wedges, then serve.

SALMON PÂTÉ

C lassy but so simple, this pâté can be served with crackers, sliced onions, and capers. You will need a food processor.

SERVES 10

2	cups salmon meat, poached and flaked (page 32)
1	cup sour cream
½	cup cream cheese
1	teaspoon dillweed
1	teaspoon salt
	Dash pepper
	Juice from ½ lemon

GARNISH:

Parsley sprigs
Lemon wedges

In a food processor combine all of the above ingredients, except garnish. Blend for 20 seconds and spoon into a ceramic bowl. Spread smooth and chill, covered with plastic wrap, for approximately 2 hours or overnight.

Garnish with lemon and parsley on top. Serve.

SEAFOOD TERRINE

A beautiful appetizer that is definitely worth the effort. Serve with crackers, onions, and capers.

SERVES 10

2 pounds raw sea scallops	½ pound crabmeat, cooked,
2 eggs	picked, and flaked
¼ cup white wine	(page 95)
Juice from ½ lemon	½ cup chopped scallions
½ pound shrimp, cooked,	Parsley, chopped
peeled, and deveined	
(page 123)	

Preheat oven to 350°F. Grease a terrine pan with butter.

Blend in food processor sea scallops, 1 egg, wine, and lemon juice for about 1 minute, until there are no big lumps showing. Scrape mixture out of food processor into small mixing bowl and set aside.

Blend shrimp and 1 egg in food processor for 15 to 20 seconds and put in a separate small mixing bowl.

Put crabmeat in another small bowl. Add 1 cup of scallop mixture to crab and blend together well.

Put shrimp mixture on bottom of terrine pan, then remaining scallop mixture in the middle. Sprinkle scallions on top of scallops and then spread crabmeat on the top. Bake for 15 to 20 minutes.

Remove from oven and let cool, then turn upside down on a serving platter. Sprinkle with parsley, cover with plastic wrap, and chill for at least 2 hours, or overnight.

CRAB LOUIS

I always run out of this dish first—it seems to be one of the old and everlasting favorites. Serve on a bed of lettuce surrounded by crackers.

SERVES 8

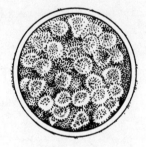

1   pound crabmeat, cooked
      and picked (see page 95)
1   8-ounce can whole tomatoes
      packed in their own juice
1   cup mayonnaise
2   dashes Tabasco sauce
1   teaspoon sugar
1   hard-boiled egg, grated

Place crabmeat in a large mixing bowl. Use your fingers to check that there is no cartilage left in the meat.

Rinse tomatoes under running water and drain all juice. Chop the tomatoes on a cutting board and rinse once again to remove any seeds.

Add the meaty tomatoes to crabmeat, then add mayonnaise, Tabasco, sugar, and egg. Blend together.

BROILED CHERRYSTONE CLAMS

An easy but impressive appetizer. For your convenience, buy the clams already shucked at your seafood store. Cherrystones are delicious raw with a little lemon juice and Cocktail Sauce (see Chapter 10), but if you'd rather cook them, broiling is another delicious way to eat them.

SERVES 4

2   dozen cherrystone clams on
      the half shell ·
6   slices bacon, cut into 4
      pieces each
    Lemon wedges

Preheat oven to 550°F (Broil).

If the clams are not shucked for you at the seafood store, rinse clams under cold running water in a colander, then shuck and place on broiler pan with a square of bacon on each clam.

Place pan on top oven rack and broil until bacon is done, approximately 5 minutes. Serve with lemon wedges.

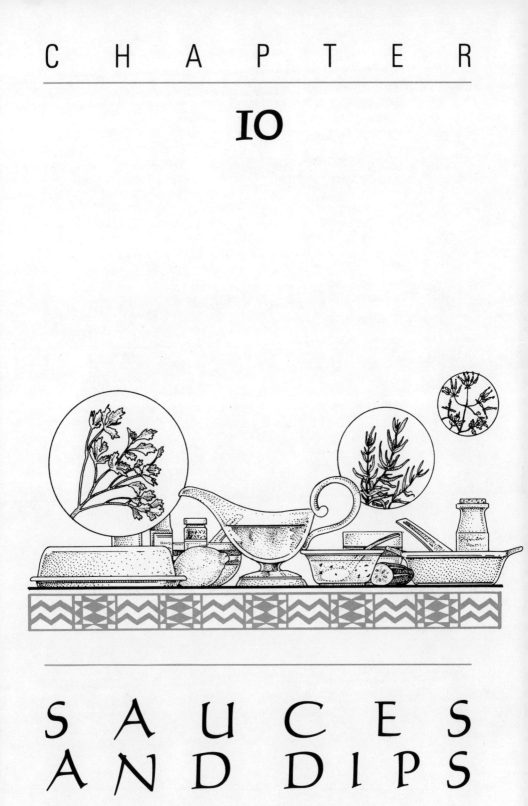

S A U C E S
A N D   D I P S

HOLLANDAISE SAUCE

MORNAY SAUCE

BUTTER SAUCE

LEMON MEUNIÈRE BUTTER

GREEN HERB BUTTER

MUSTARD SAUCE

COCKTAIL SAUCE

TARTAR SAUCE

RAZOR CLAM DIP

SPICY CRAB DIP

HOLLANDAISE SAUCE

This is a very touchy sauce and likes to separate, so follow the directions carefully.

MAKES 1 CUP

½   cup butter
3   egg yolks
1½ tablespoons fresh lemon
        juice

In a saucepan melt butter over low heat, being careful not to brown, and set aside.

In a double boiler, over medium heat, using hot water (not boiling water), whisk egg yolk briskly until thick and creamy. Be careful not to let the bottom of the pan touch the surface of the water in the pan below. Slowly add butter and lemon juice, alternating them and constantly stirring.

Keep the sauce warm until ready to serve.

MORNAY SAUCE

MAKES 2 CUPS

¼ cup butter
1 medium onion, minced
¼ cup flour
1 cup milk
2 egg yolks

¼ cup cream
¼ cup grated Parmesan cheese
¼ cup grated Gruyère cheese

In a heavy saucepan melt butter over low heat, add onion and sauté until soft. Add flour and mix thoroughly. Slowly add milk, stirring constantly, until it thickens slightly (like creamy soup).

Beat the egg yolks and cream together. Slowly add a little of the sauce to the yolk and cream mixture, stirring rapidly so that the sauce doesn't cook the egg. Then add the entire yolk mixture to the sauce, followed by the cheese, stirring constantly over low heat, until sauce is thickened. This sauce may be then baked in your recipe or covered and kept warm. It is best to make this sauce as soon as possible before serving; it may lose some of its silky smooth texture and you risk the chance of burning if you try to keep it warm for a long period of time.

BUTTER SAUCE

Butter sauces are best with poached, grilled, or broiled seafood.

MAKES ½ CUP

½ cup butter
    5–6 cloves garlic, pressed
1   tablespoon minced fresh
      parsley
1   teaspoon lemon juice
1½ tablespoons grated
      Parmesan cheese

In a saucepan melt the butter with the garlic over low heat until fragrant and foamy. Be careful not to let the butter brown. Add parsley and lemon juice. Stir. Add cheese and mix together. Serve.

This sauce may be made in advance, only do not add the cheese until the last minute, when you are heating the sauce to serve.

LEMON MEUNIÈRE BUTTER

MAKES ½ CUP

½   cup butter
2   tablespoons minced fresh
      parsley
2   tablespoons lemon juice

In a saucepan melt butter over low heat until fragrant and foamy. Add parsley and lemon juice. Stir well and serve.

If you like a slightly bitter taste, let the butter brown a little and then add the parsley and lemon juice.

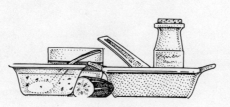

GREEN HERB BUTTER

This sauce is delicious when spooned over plain fish. It easily turns simple fish into an extraordinary meal.

MAKES ½ CUP

½ cup butter	1 teaspoon dried tarragon
2 shallots, minced	1 teaspoon garlic powder
1 scallion, finely chopped	1 teaspoon dried chervil
1 teaspoon lemon juice	1 teaspoon dried parsley
1 tablespoon sherry	

In a saucepan melt butter with all other ingredients over low heat until the shallots are translucent, approximately 5 minutes. Serve warm.

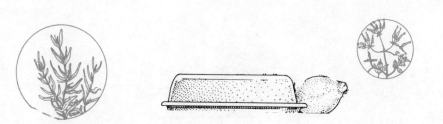

MUSTARD SAUCE

Nice with cracked crabmeat.

MAKES ABOUT 1¼ CUPS

¼ cup finely minced onion
2 tablespoons Dijon mustard
3 teaspoons sugar
¼ cup peanut oil (or a light
   sesame oil for a unique
   taste)

¼ cup cider or white vinegar
2 tablespoons sour cream
4 eggs, hard-boiled, minced

In a bowl combine all ingredients and mix thoroughly. Serve chilled.

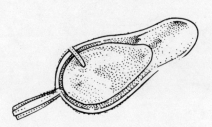

COCKTAIL SAUCE

The best cocktail sauce I've ever had. The horseradish gives it extra zing! If you desire a hotter sauce or a milder one, adjust by using more or less Tabasco and horseradish.

MAKES 1½ CUPS

1   cup ketchup
1   tablespoon lemon juice
1   tablespoon orange juice
    (optional)

2   tablespoons horseradish
2   dashes Tabasco sauce
2   dashes Worcestershire sauce

In a bowl mix all ingredients together thoroughly and keep refrigerated until ready to serve.

TARTAR SAUCE

Tartar sauce originally came from Mongolian Tartars (a tribal race in Russia). It is now an American seafood staple and is perfect with fried food.

MAKES 1 CUP

1   cup mayonnaise
1   teaspoon minced fresh
    parsley
½   teaspoon finely chopped
    capers
1   tablespoon finely minced
    sweet dill pickle,
    drained, or use pickle
    relish

Squeeze of lemon juice
Salt and freshly ground
    white pepper to taste

In a bowl combine all ingredients. Chill for 2 hours or more, covered.

RAZOR CLAM DIP

Although this recipe calls for razor clams, they are often difficult to find. Cherrystone clams may be substituted. This is a fresh approach to a traditional clam dip.

MAKES 1½ CUPS

1 cup minced cooked razor or cherrystone clams, well drained (page 172)	¼ cup finely chopped scallions
1 3-ounce package cream cheese, room temperature	1 tablespoon Worcestershire sauce
	¼ cup sour cream
	1 teaspoon garlic salt

In a bowl mix all ingredients until well blended, saving a few chopped scallions for a garnish. Serve at room temperature.

SPICY CRAB DIP

A spicy version of Razor Clam Dip.

MAKES 2 CUPS

2 3-ounce packages cream
   cheese, room
   temperature
¼ cup light cream (milk may
   be substituted)
1 tablespoon soy sauce
1 tablespoon wine vinegar

½ cup cooked and picked
   crabmeat (page 95)
Pinch cayenne pepper
½ teaspoon garlic powder
Pinch chili powder
¼ cup chopped onions

Preheat oven to 550°F (Broil).

Blend cream cheese with cream, soy sauce, and vinegar. When well blended, add remaining ingredients, except onions.

Brown onions under broiler until slightly burnt. Cool and add the dip. Serve at room temperature.

SOUPS AND CHOWDERS

BASIC FISH STOCK OR FISH FUMET

Fish stock or fumet is a reduced water- and wine-based fish stock used for sauces and rich soups.

MAKES ABOUT 1¼–1½ QUARTS

6 cups water	1 small bouquet garni
2 cups dry white wine	(parsley, thyme sprig,
1 medium onion	and bay leaf tied in a
1 medium carrot	small piece of
1 tablespoon butter	cheesecloth)
3 pounds trimmings (heads	½ teaspoon salt
and bones, no skins, and	3 white peppercorns
gills removed)	

In a large covered stockpot, bring water and wine to a boil. Add remaining ingredients, reduce heat, and gently simmer for 15 minutes. Be careful not to cook the stock too long, or you will have a completed stock with a pronounced flavor of fish bones.

Strain stock, do not press or squeeze trimmings or stock may become cloudy. You are now ready to use your stock in your recipe or to freeze it to use at any time.

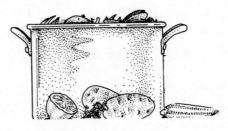

COURT BOUILLON

Used to poach fish and enhance the flavor of the completed dish. The salt content in the bouillon is useful when firming the flesh of soft-textured fish.

MAKES 2 QUARTS

5 cups water
2 cups dry white wine
1 large onion
1 medium carrot
1 leek

1 small bouquet garni (parsley, thyme sprig, and bay leaf tied in a small piece of cheesecloth)
2 teaspoons salt
8 white peppercorns

In a large covered stockpot, bring water and wine to a boil. Add all remaining ingredients except peppercorns, simmer over medium-low heat for 10 minutes, then add peppercorns and simmer for 10 minutes more. Strain bouillon, and it is now ready to use in your favorite recipe or to freeze for future use. (If you are using the bouillon for an aspic glaze recipe, make sure the bouillon is strained well so that your glaze will be clear.)

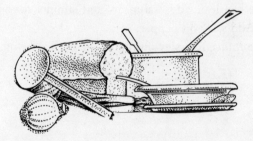

CRAB GUMBO

Gumbo, the traditional French Creole dish, tastes even better with fish than the traditional chicken. I like to serve pearl barley or rice with this meal. You can either spoon it into the gumbo or eat it on the side.

SERVES 6

2 teaspoons butter	4 large tomatoes, peeled and
1 cup chopped onions	chopped (about 1½ to 2
3 cloves garlic, finely	cups)
chopped	½ cup tomato juice
2 tablespoons flour	1 bay leaf
2 cups Fish Stock (page 178)	1 pound crabmeat, cooked
3 cups sliced okra	and picked (page 95)
	Salt and pepper to taste
	Parsley, minced

In a sauté pan melt butter over medium-low heat. Sauté onions and garlic until lightly browned. Add flour and mix until well blended and there are no lumps. Add stock, vegetables, tomato juice, and bay leaf; bring to a boil. Reduce heat and simmer, covered, for 30 minutes.

Remove bay leaf, add crabmeat, and simmer for another 10 to 15 minutes. Add salt and pepper.

Sprinkle minced parsley on top of the gumbo before serving.

CRAB AND MUSHROOM BISQUE

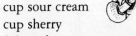

A great creamy wintertime soup. Garnish the individual bowls with parsley.

SERVES 6–8

½	cup butter	2	cups milk
2	cloves pressed garlic	¾	cup sour cream
2	tablespoons minced shallots	¼	cup sherry
			Salt and pepper to taste
1	pound fresh mushrooms, thinly sliced	1	pound crabmeat, cooked and picked (page 95)
2	cups Fish Fumet (page 178) or chicken stock	2	tablespoons minced fresh parsley

In a sauté pan melt butter over low heat and add garlic, shallots, and mushrooms until soft. Transfer to a deep, large soup pot.

Turn heat to medium and add fumet, milk, sour cream, sherry, salt and pepper.

Stirring constantly, bring to a boil. Reduce that, add crabmeat, and simmer gently uncovered for 15 minutes, then cover until ready to serve. Garnish with parsley.

SHRIMP-TOMATO BISQUE

G reat to serve before dinner, or as a meal all by itself.

SERVES 6–8

1	8-ounce can Italian plum tomatoes packed in juice, coarsley chopped, seeds discarded	1	pound shrimp, peeled and deveined (page 123)
¼	cup butter	2	cups heavy cream
1	cup chopped onions	2	tablespoons flour
2	cups Fish Fumet (page 178) or chicken stock	2	tablespoons tomato paste
½	cup white wine		Salt and pepper to taste
		2	tablespoons minced fresh parsley

In a strainer drain tomatoes and run under cold water.

In a large soup pot melt butter over low heat and sauté onions until they are translucent but not brown. Add tomatoes, fish fumet, and wine. Bring to a boil. Add shrimp and cook for 1 to 2 minutes, depending on size of shrimp. Be careful not to overcook. The shrimp will cook when you simmer the soup.

In a bowl, add cream and mix flour and tomato paste into it, until well blended.

Reduce heat under soup pot and slowly stir in cream mixture. Season with salt and pepper. Cover and let simmer for 10 to 15 minutes.

Serve with parsley sprinkled on top for a tasty touch of color.

CHILLED CLAM AND TOMATO SOUP

Serve this soup very cold and garnish with the lemon slices either hung around the edge of the bowl or floating on top.

SERVES 4

3   cups tomato juice
1   cup cooked clams, cut into
        bite-size pieces (page
        109)
1   teaspoon lemon juice
1   cup reserved clam broth,
        or 2 8-ounce bottles
½   teaspoon garlic salt

GARNISH:

Green scallions, chopped
Thin lemon slices

In a saucepan simmer tomato juice, clams, lemon juice, clam broth and garlic salt for 15 minutes. Cool, then chill.

Garnish with scallions and lemon slices. Serve.

CORN AND BACON CLAM CHOWDER

A new version of pure Americana.

SERVES 6–8

5	slices bacon, cooked crisp and crumbled	2	cups chopped cooked clams (page 109)
½	cup chopped celery	1	teaspoon salt
2	medium onions, chopped	½	teaspoon white pepper
2	cups diced potatoes	½	teaspoon freshly ground black pepper, plus extra for garnish
1	cup clam juice		
1	cup kernel corn		Butter
3	cups milk		
2	tablespoons flour		

In a heavy skillet fry bacon until crisp. Set bacon to one side to cool, then crumble.

Over medium heat sauté celery and onions in bacon grease until soft, 3 to 4 minutes.

Put celery, onions, and bacon grease in a large pot. Add potatoes and clam juice liquid and simmer over medium-low heat until potatoes are tender, about 15 minutes. Add crumbled bacon, corn, milk, flour, clams, salt, and peppers. Cover and let simmer for 15 to 20 minutes, stirring frequently.

When ready to serve, top with a pat of butter and freshly ground pepper.

NEW ENGLAND CLAM CHOWDER

Traditional, hearty, delicious, this staple is great served with warm biscuits.

SERVES 8

¼ cup butter	4½ cups milk
2 cloves garlic, pressed	1 pound cleaned razor
1½ cups diced onions	clams, or 1½ cups
1 cup thinly sliced celery	chopped cherrystone
¼ cup flour	clams
2 cups finely diced potatoes	Pinch thyme
½ cup clam juice	Salt and pepper to taste

In a large kettle melt butter over medium heat and sauté garlic, onions, and celery until onions are translucent. Remove from heat and add flour, coating onions and celery.

Return to heat and add potatoes and clam juice. Simmer over medium heat until potatoes are tender, about 10 minutes. Add milk, clams, and seasonings. Simmer until clams are thoroughly cooked, approximately 10 minutes uncovered.

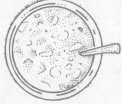

KACHEMAK BAY SEAFOOD CHOWDER

This is a chowder that will warm any fisherman after a day out in the brisk Alaskan waters.

SERVES 8

6⅓	cups water	1	bay leaf
1½	cups uncooked pasta shells	5	tablespoons flour
¼	cup butter	1	1-pound halibut fillet, cubed into 1″ pieces
½	cup chopped onions	½	cup diced green pepper
½	cup chopped celery	6	oysters, shucked
1	clove garlic, minced	1	cup light cream
⅓	cup dry white wine	½	pound medium-size shrimp, peeled and deveined
2	cups Fish Broth (page 178)		
1	teaspoon salt	¼	cup chopped fresh parsley
½	teaspoon dried thyme	¼	cup chopped pimientoes
½	teaspoon grated nutmeg	¼	pound scallops
½	teaspoon pepper		

In a pot bring 4 cups water to a boil and cook pasta until tender. Drain and set aside.

In a large saucepan melt butter over medium-low heat and sauté onions, celery, and garlic for about 5 minutes. Add wine, fish broth, 2 cups water, and seasonings; raise heat to medium. Cover and simmer for 15 minutes.

In a bowl mix flour with ⅓ cup cold water to a smooth paste, stirring constantly. Add to simmering liquid and cook for another 15 minutes, uncovered, stirring frequently. Add halibut cubes, green peppers, and oysters. Simmer uncovered for 10 to 15 minutes more.

Remove bay leaf. Stir in pasta shells, light cream, shrimp, scallops, parsley, and pimientoes. Heat slowly over medium heat to simmering again and serve.

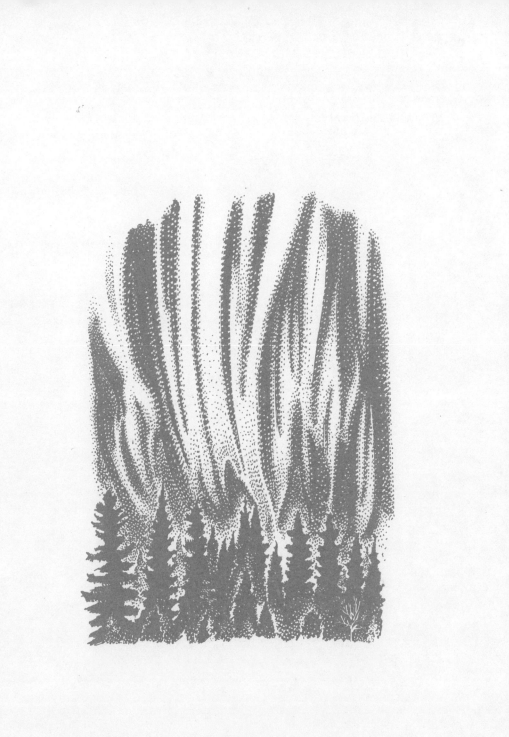

CHAPTER

12

BRUNCHES

SALMON QUICHE

HALIBUT SALAD

CRAB TARTS

ALASKAN OMELET

CRAB-FILLED AVOCADO

EGGS OSCAR

MARINATED SCALLOP AND ASPARAGUS SALAD
WITH LIME-GINGER DRESSING

SHRIMP-STUFFED TOMATOES

MEXICAN SHRIMP SALAD

COLD TARRAGON SALMON WITH VEGETABLES

SALMON QUICHE

Real men eat this quiche and love it! Since you can make it the night before, it's great if you need something that can be made ahead of time.

SERVES 6–8

PASTRY SHELL

1 ⅓   cups all-purpose flour
½   cup butter
2–3   teaspoons cold white wine (water may be substituted)
1   egg, separated

FILLING

2   cups milk
½   cup flaked, poached salmon (page 32)
½   cup grated Swiss cheese
3   eggs
Dash each salt, white pepper, grated nutmeg, dried chives

Preheat oven to 375°F.

To make shell, put flour in a large mixing bowl and cut in butter until mixture resembles coarse meal, or small peas. Add wine and egg yolk and mix thoroughly. Press into an 8″ quiche dish or pie plate.

Brush pastry shell with egg white and prick holes in crust using a fork (approximately 3 times on the bottom and 5 times around the sides).

To make filling, pour milk into a saucepan and scald. Set aside to cool.

Meanwhile, sprinkle salmon and cheese on bottom of pastry.

In a bowl mix milk, eggs, and seasonings together. Pour mixture into pastry shell. Bake for 30 to 40 minutes. The quiche will be slightly brown on top and an inserted knife will come out clean when done.

HALIBUT SALAD

One of my favorite recipes, it was also very popular in my seafood store in Anchorage. I could barely make it fast enough to keep it in stock.

Many of my customers spread it in sandwiches, on crackers, put it in a salad, or used it in making all kinds of hors d'oeuvres. The way *I* like it best is straight out of the bowl! If you save the roast and parts around the head of the halibut, it would be perfect for this salad.

MAKES 3 CUPS

2 cups cooked halibut meat, boned and flaked (page 32)	1 teaspoon minced fresh parsley
½ cup finely chopped celery	1 teaspoon lemon juice
½ cup finely chopped onions	1 cup mayonnaise
3 scallions, finely chopped	2 tablespoons chopped dillweed

In a large mixing bowl combine halibut, celery, onion, scallions, parsley, and lemon juice. Add mayonnaise and dillweed. Mix thoroughly and serve.

SERVING SUGGESTION: Nice garnishes for the halibut salad are parsley sprigs, cherry tomatoes, lemon slices, and a sprinkle of dillweed.

CRAB TARTS

The Queen of Hearts would have loved these tarts—they are worth a king's ransom.

SERVES 3–4

1   recipe pastry shell dough (see Salmon Quiche, page 192)
4   egg yolks
2   cups milk
1   pound crabmeat, cooked and picked (page 95)

5   scallions, chopped
1   tablespoon lemon juice
1   teaspoon salt
1   teaspoon pepper
2   cloves garlic, pressed

Preheat oven to 375°F.

Roll pastry dough so it is ¼" thick, and press into cupcake tins or individual tart dishes.

In a large bowl lightly beat eggs and milk together until they are well blended but not foamy. Mix in the remaining ingredients.

Fill tart shells with crab mixture. Bake for 20 to 30 minutes, or until a knife inserted comes out clean.

ALASKAN OMELET

Move over Western, Spanish and plain old ham and cheese—here comes a great Alaskan omelet!

SERVES 2

1   tablespoon butter
3   eggs, well beaten
2   tablespoons sour cream
½   cup cooked and picked
    crabmeat (page 95)
2   tablespoons chopped
    scallions

Use a small omelet pan or small round sauté pan to melt the butter over a medium heat. Add eggs and rotate the pan to coat it evenly with eggs. Depending on pan you use, it will take 30 seconds to a minute for eggs to cook.

Transfer eggs to a warm plate, which helps to keep the omelet fluffy. Spread half with sour cream, crabmeat, and scallions. The warmth of the omelet will heat the crabmeat and the sour cream. Reserve a few scallions to sprinkle on top.

Fold over and serve immediately.

CRAB-FILLED AVOCADO

If your avocados are not ripe, put them in a brown paper bag at room temperature for a day or two before making this recipe.

SERVES 4

1 ½   cups cooked and picked
        crabmeat (page 95)
½   cup mayonnaise
1   tablespoon capers
2   eggs, hard-boiled and
        chopped
2   large ripe avocados, sliced
        in half lengthwise,
        seeds removed
1   tomato, thinly sliced
¼   cup shredded Swiss cheese

Preheat oven to 550°F (Broil).

In a medium-size mixing bowl combine crabmeat, mayonnaise, capers, and eggs. When well blended, fill avocado halves with the mixture.

Top with 1 slice of tomato, then with 1 tablespoon shredded cheese. Place under the broiler just long enough to melt the cheese, approximately 30 seconds to 1 minute. Serve immediately.

EGGS OSCAR

This dish is similar to eggs Benedict, but it substitutes crabmeat for the Canadian bacon.

For brunch, I like to serve these eggs with asparagus spears and fresh melon.

SERVES 3

3	English muffins, halved	2	tablespoons vinegar (optional)
1½	cups cooked and picked crabmeat (page 95)	1	recipe Hollandaise Sauce (page 166)
6	eggs		Paprika
2½	cups water (optional)		

Lightly toast muffins and put 2 halves on each plate. Add ¼ cup crabmeat on top of each muffin.

In an egg poacher poach eggs to your desired timing and place on top of the crab and muffin. If you don't have an egg poacher, in a large saucepan bring water to a boil, add vinegar, and bring to a boil again. Carefully crack eggs into water, bring careful not to break yolks. Cook for approximately 2 minutes and remove from water with a slotted spoon.

Gently pat eggs dry and spoon hollandaise sauce on top. Sprinkle with a touch of paprika and serve immediately so sauce doesn't cool and separate.

MARINATED SCALLOP AND ASPARAGUS SALAD WITH LIME-GINGER DRESSING

This is a nice dish to serve for a light luncheon dinner on a hot day.

SERVES 4–6

1 pound sea scallops, well rinsed	**LIME-GINGER DRESSING:**
1 cup lime juice	
1 teaspoon ground ginger	Juice of 3 lemons
	¾ cup salad oil
	Pinch ground ginger
	Salt and pepper to taste
	24 asparagus stalks
	1 large head lettuce, or 2 small, leaves separated
	1 medium red onion, chopped
	2 tomatoes, cut into wedges

In a small glass bowl marinate the scallops in lime juice and ginger for at least 1 hour. The lime juice will "cook" the scallops. In a bowl or jar mix the dressing ingredients.

In a pot of enough water to cover, steam asparagus until tender but not overdone, 4 to 6 minutes.

On each plate arrange lettuce leaves, then asparagus, onion, tomatoes, and marinated scallops.

Spoon dressing over the top and serve.

SHRIMP-STUFFED TOMATOES

You can bake the tomatoes in advance of serving, let them cool, and refrigerate them to serve chilled.

SERVES 4

4   large tomatoes
1   pound medium-size shrimp,
       peeled, deveined, and
       cooked (page 123)
2   egg whites
1   tablespoon ground ginger
1   tablespoon white wine
2   tablespoons cornstarch
4   scallions, finely chopped

Preheat oven to 350°F. Lightly grease a casserole or pie plate.

Cut stem from top of each tomato and very carefully remove all seeds and meat, leaving a firm shell.

In a mixing bowl combine remaining ingredients.

Fill tomatoes with shrimp mixture and place in the casserole or pie plate. Bake on the middle rack of your oven for 25 to 30 minutes, until golden on top and firm in center.

MEXICAN SHRIMP SALAD

When you feel like having a salad for lunch or dinner on a hot day, this is perfect. Serve immediately so that the chips and lettuce stay crisp and the chop meat is still warm.

SERVES 8

1   head iceberg lettuce, leaves separated
2   large tomatoes, coarsely chopped
2   medium avocados, coarsely chopped
2   large white onions, diced
1   small bunch scallions, chopped
1   6-ounce can chopped green chiles

1   16-ounce can dark kidney beans, drained, rinsed
1   cup grated Cheddar cheese
2   cups cooked cocktail shrimp
1   pound chop meat
1   ¾-pound bag corn chips, broken into small pieces
1   teaspoon garlic powder
    Thousand Island dressing

In a large salad bowl toss together the lettuce, tomatoes, avocados, onions, scallions, chiles, kidney beans, cheese, and shrimp. Refrigerate.

In a large skillet brown the chop meat with garlic powder over high heat. Drain off excess grease.

Toss meat and chips with salad. Top with salad dressing.

Toss thoroughly and serve immediately.

COLD TARRAGON SALMON WITH VEGETABLES

Tarragon, a spice often used in French cuisine, is a perfect accent for salmon.

SERVES 6

TARRAGON MARINADE:

1	cup olive oil
½	cup tarragon vinegar (found in specialty food stores)
	Juice from ½ lemon
2	tablespoons pressed garlic
1	small Bermuda onion, minced
1	teaspoon salt
1	tablespoon sugar
¼	teaspoon dried tarragon

6	small new potatoes, boiled then halved
	Lettuce leaves
1	1-pound salmon fillet, poached (page 32) and chilled
1	large tomato, sliced
1	avocado, sliced
1	cucumber, sliced
	Capers

In a large mixing bowl combine marinade ingredients. Whisk until thoroughly blended.

Pour marinade over potatoes then cover and refrigerate for several hours. Drain and reserve marinade.

Arrange lettuce on bottom of plate. Slice poached salmon into serving-size pieces and place in center of plate. Then arrange potatoes, tomato, avocado, and cucumber on sides of salmon.

Sprinkle top of salmon with capers for garnish. Serve with reserved marinade on the side.

D I N N E R
M E N U
SUGGESTIONS

Here are some seafood menu suggestions for dinners ranging from casual family-style dinners to elegant entertaining for friends.

CASUAL DINNERS FOR 4 TO 6

Sring Dinner

POACHED SALMON WITH ORANGE SAUCE (PAGE 31)
FRESH STEAMED ASPARAGUS
TOSSED SALAD WITH VINAIGRETTE DRESSING
FRUIT COMPOTE

Summer Barbecue

SPICY GRILLED SALMON STEAKS (PAGE 29)
CORN ON THE COB
SLICED BEEFSTEAK OR JERSEY TOMATOES
WATERMELON

Indoor Picnic

BEER-BATTERED HALIBUT (PAGE 60)
COLESLAW
TOSSED SALAD WITH SWEET AND SOUR OR VINAIGRETTE DRESSING
HOMEMADE CHOCOLATE CHIP COOKIES WITH ICE CREAM

Easy Oriental Dinner

SWEET AND SOUR SHRIMP (PAGE 129)
STEAMED WHITE RICE
STEAMED BROCCOLI
FRESH PINEAPPLE CHUNKS

LIGHT DINNERS FOR 4 TO 6

CLASSIC

POACHED HALIBUT WITH SHRIMP SAUCE (PAGE 58)
ASPARAGUS SPEARS
FRESH FRUIT

SAVORY

STEAMED CRAB WITH DEVILED BUTTER (PAGE 94—DOUBLE RECIPE)
TOSSED SALAD WITH VINAIGRETTE
ORANGE SECTIONS IN GRAND MARNIER

HEARTY SOUP AND SALAD

NEW ENGLAND CLAM CHOWDER (PAGE 185)
BAKING POWDER BISCUITS
TOSSED SALAD WITH OLIVE OIL AND BALSAMIC VINEGAR
GREEN APPLE TART

ELEGANT ENTERTAINING FOR 4 TO 6

Sophisticated Seafood Dinner

SALMON PÂTÉ (PAGE 156) OR
CRAB AND MUSHROOM BISQUE (PAGE 181)
SCALLOP QUENELLES WITH SHRIMP SAUCE (PAGE 88—DOUBLE RECIPE)
ASPARAGUS SPEARS STEAMED WITH BUTTER
TOSSED SALAD WITH OLIVE OIL AND LEMON DRESSING
ORANGE SECTIONS IN GRAND MARNIER

Fancy Summer Feast

CLAMS CASINO (PAGE 155) OR
SHRIMP-TOMATO BISQUE (PAGE 182)
SALMON ON ASPARAGUS WITH HOLLANDAISE (PAGE 49)
TOSSED SALAD AND VINAIGRETTE DRESSING
CHOCOLATE TORTE

Light and Classy

OYSTERS ON THE HALF SHELL OR
CHILLED CLAM AND TOMATO SOUP (PAGE 183)
SEAFOOD SOUFFLÉ (PAGE 138)
TOSSED SALAD
FRESH FRUIT SLICES
ICE CREAM OR SORBET

ENTERTAINING 6 TO 8, BUFFET-STYLE

CRAB LOUIS (PAGE 158)
HALIBUT SALAD WITH CRACKERS (PAGE 193)
WHOLE SALMON STUFFED WITH WILD RICE (PAGE 33)
TOSSED SALAD
STEAMED ASSORTED VEGETABLES WITH BUTTER
COOKIES

CRAB TARTS (PAGE 194—DOUBLE RECIPE)
CLAMS CASINO (PAGE 155)
COLD SALMON IN ASPIC (PAGE 38)
BOILED NEW POTATOES IN BUTTER SAUCE (PAGE 166—DOUBLE THE
RECIPE)
MASHED SWEET POTATOES
TOSSED SALAD
FRESH BERRIES WITH WHIPPED CREAM

BOILED SHRIMP WITH COCKTAIL SAUCE (PAGE 170)
RED PEPPERS AND SCALLOPS IN RICE (PAGE 86)
STEAMED BROCCOLI AND BUTTER SAUCE (PAGE 166—DOUBLE THE
RECIPE)
CAESAR SALAD
FRUIT COMPOTE

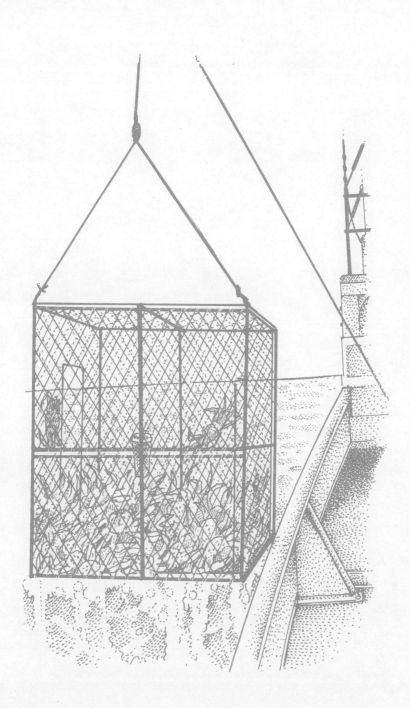

INDEX

ABOUT THE AUTHOR

Linette Hoglund lived in Alaska for almost two years, during which time she ran a family-owned seafood store, Jewel Lake Seafood. She catered fresh seafood to restaurants and gourmet food stores; this led to her culinary interests and consequently to this book.

Now living in New York, Ms. Hoglund is the youngest female broker on the New York Stock Exchange. She remains active in the cooking field, preparing her recipes for friends and special catered affairs.